Managing the Sense of a Region

Managing the Sense of a Region

Kevin Lynch

The MIT Press
Cambridge, Massachusetts, and London, England

This book was set in IBM Baskerville by Techdata Associates Inc., and printed on R & E Book and bound in Columbia MBL-4610 by Murray Printing Company in the United States of America.

Library of Congress Cataloging in Publication Data

Lynch, Kevin.
 Managing the sense of a region.

 Includes bibliographies and index.
 1. Regional planning—Environmental aspects—United States. I. Title.
HT392.L95   309.2'5'0973   76-26626
ISBN 0-262-12072-0

Contents

List of Illustrations

1 Mission Valley as it was and is.

Managing the Sense of a Region

Twenty years ago Mission Valley was open countryside, passing through the city of San Diego like a broad green river in that arid urban landscape. Houses looked over the high bluffs on either side. On the valley floor there were dairy farms, strung along the line of trees that marked the little stream.

Now the valley is a breathtaking giant shopping strip, with its freeway, parking lots, offices, stadium, two major shopping centers, and a yard for old car bodies. The stream itself is no longer visible (but given a flood, it may show to better advantage). The bluffs are scraped bare. There is a new smell to the air. The sounds have changed, and the asphalt surfaces reflect the heat. This is a walk we can take in the valley today:

a   b

2a-f In the valley among the cars.

c

2 *(continued)*

d

e

f

San Diegans have not forgotten the way the valley was, nor do they lack for feelings about the way it is. But they use the shops frequently, and thousands of commuters, from inland and the north, drive through the valley every day. The story of this change is not unusual for any North American city. It is a tale of locating a new freeway, of a shift in the central business district to meet parking demands and urban growth, of large land profits, tax windfalls, a zoning battle, and a brief, belated, isolated, "unreasonable" resistance.

Judging this event by hindsight, planners will discuss the role of the automobile, the future of shopping and of the central business district, the issues of urban growth, the economics of land speculation, and municipal reliance on the real estate tax. They are important issues, though a touch abstract, as is usual in planning talk. But in the end, these issues reduce to the quality of life, at least for someone, since without that quality there is no need for economics, taxation, cities, and all the rest.

It is surprising, then, that in a technical discussion of Mission Valley very little time will be devoted to analyzing how the new environment affects the everyday lives of the people who use it— that is, how it affects them in an immediate sense, through their eyes, ears, nose, and skin. Many planners will consider this analysis too obvious to dally over or, if not obvious, then trivial—too unpredictable and too personal to be part of any public discussion. But those who sense the place do not agree, and their complaints are stable, specific, and consistent. Moreover, the issue is not as simple or as obvious as it may seem.

Even when carried out according to careful planning, such transformations as the Mission Valley gala are evaluated and determined on the grounds of economics, transportation, politics, space requirements, landownership, and ecology. Once a location decision is made, an enlightened city government or a developer may then turn to some professional to make the thing beautiful. But the human experience of the landscape is as fundamental as any of those other factors and should be considered from the first.

I mean to take the peculiar position that the experiential quality of the environment must be planned for at a regional scale, since Mission Valleys occur for regional reasons, and people now live their lives at that scale. But to talk of deliberately planning or managing the sensory quality of a large region raises three immediate questions:

What do we mean by sensory quality?

Does it have any real social importance?

Can it actually be managed at a regional scale?

Sensuous (or sensory) quality refers to the look, sound, smell, and feel of a place. Despite the popular overtones of the term, it does not refer to any sinful or voluptuous dimension.

The social importance of these qualities is frequently overlooked or denied. I shall argue that they are of vital concern to sensing beings. Plans that ignore them make disheartening cities.

The last question is the most difficult one. Sensory quality is infrequently considered at a city or regional scale and rarely with success. It is thought to be something one cares for only in designing plazas or important buildings. On the contrary, I think it must be considered in planning for an entire inhabited region, and for the everyday environment experienced in the whole range of daily action. This essay will attempt to substantiate that conviction. But since this is a possibility more than an actual achievement, there will be room for denial.

Even so, *should* sensory quality be so managed? Design of the large-scale environment and concern for its esthetic or sensuous form have in the past usually been the act of a dominating power. Centralized governments built Peking, baroque Rome, and Haussmann's Paris. The American "city beautiful" movement flourished at a time when upper-class citizens still had some control of city politics, and it reflected their tastes. Designing the physical setting of a large institution has often been a matter of imposing a monumental form on a multitude of unwilling users.

The linkage between design and centralized power, however, is not inevitable. I shall assume that a public agency should be committed not only to fitting the environment to the needs of its users but also to giving them control of it wherever possible. This assumption leads to choices of strategy and technique not usually associated with large-scale environmental design.

In the United States, concern with the sensory quality of regions has grown from two roots, from which in turn sprang two separate trees of professional knowledge and activity. The older one began with architecture and landscape architecture in the service of kings, and this art was then employed by public bodies or large corporations that were building parks or monumental places, as in the "city beautiful" movement. Lately, this professional effort has spread to other, more ordinary locations: housing projects, new towns, and urban renewal areas. However, these are projects that still require a large-scale change managed by some powerful agent. The emphasis of the tradition is on urban sites, on the detailed control of form, on an intuitive assessment by experts, on creative design, on submission to the "realities of development" (that is, to the motives and means of those who have the power to decide), on an extension of the principles and working methods of architecture, and very often on a predilection for bigness *(61, 146).** Yet the experience of work in urban places has also in time brought some awareness of the plurality of clients and of the conflicts of politics. The recent "urban design plans" for some of our large cities are new branches of this same tree *(13, 20, 23, 29, 33, 35, 39, 45).*

The younger plant is rooted in land management, particularly within the national forests, where emphasis is shifting from tim-

_____
*Italicized numbers correspond to item numbers in the bibliographies.

bering to recreation on a mass scale. Here the professionals are concerned with rural—not urban—land, with the preservation of natural beauty rather than the creation of something, and with management more than design. The managing agency is stable and completely controls a large area. The professional emphasis has been correspondingly technical and systematic. It carries over from timber management a strong reliance on quantitative technique, rational optima, and well-defined, explicit measures of "goodness," such as the number of users or the visibility of water *(18, 19, 36, 38, 41, 44, 47, 49)*. This forest viewpoint has very naturally allied itself with the concern over pollution of the air, the water, and the land. The attitudes are similarly clustered around nature, conservation, scientific analysis, and technical rationality. The drive to preserve fine historic man-made settings and the growing interest in maintaining traditional rural scenery add other voices to this same chorus. While the criteria of historic and scenic preservation may seem less "scientific," they strive in the same way to move toward what is firm and universal.

Each tradition can learn from the other. (The author comes from the first of these traditions and is trying to reform.) Design and management are not incompatible or even clearly separable. Similarly, systematic rationality and creative intuition are not irreconcilable. Whether a site is urban or rural, and whether its management is single or plural, rich or poor, will affect the techniques and criteria to be used. But there are common underlying principles and methods of design and analysis. We can deal with problems other than forests, parks, historic areas, or central business districts. These two traditions should be fused and so gain the competence to deal with a more inclusive range of issues. The unifying theme should be the way that the sense of a region affects the lives of its people. Later, perhaps, we may even grow to the point where we can think of its influence on other lives—of animals and perhaps even plants. For the present, an effective, broad, human concern would be a giant step.

Appendix 1 contains a brief review of recent U.S. experience in planning for the sensory quality of large areas, making reference to actual studies and to review articles. At the city scale, where the problem is most acute, the list of studies is not long, and the list of achievements is even shorter. Indeed, the quality of the urban environment is patently poor throughout most of the world. Places generally thought desirable are usually the remnants of a process of slow development, which occurred within sharp constraints of natural condition and cultural limitation and since then have been enriched by continuous habitation and reformation (old farming areas, historic cities). Or, if not, they are those places less frequently encountered, where the design was closely fitted to the requirements of the persons who were to use them and who had some power to affect the outcome (private gardens, some upper-middle-class housing areas, some shopping centers).

Our lack of achievement in environmental design is not inevitable, but it is not due to some easily exorcised cause, such as a lack of money, public apathy, errors in administrative structure, or political intrigue. One root difficulty is the divorce of the users of a place from control over its shape and management, which leads to inappropriate form and the imposition of alien purposes. Another is our inability to control real estate development, due above all to the chaos of local government and to the private exploitation of land. These are not simple problems: they go to the heart of our political, economic, and social structure. This essay can only allude to them, while discussing the positions that a regional planning staff can realistically take in the United States today.

A further difficulty is our lack of understanding of the direct effects of the environment on human beings and of how to control those effects to suit our rather vague, and certainly complex, purposes. We are inexperienced and burdened with outworn attitudes. This essay deals primarily with these latter problems, although it cannot ignore the others. While trying to specify how we can use what we already know about environmental quality, it will also expose the limits of our knowledge. Some references to the sources of the available evidence are collected in the Bibliography of Research.

The Sensory Quality of Regions

It is a puzzle to find some simple word for the sensed quality of a place. There are fine words for the separate sensations: look, sound, touch, smell. But if we speak of the senses in general, we are left among the ghosts of old controversies in psychology and ethics. "Sensuous" is the correct term, but only academic people can overlook its overtones of lewdness and luxuriance. Apparently coined by John Milton to circumvent those very connotations of the earlier word "sensual," the term itself now strays toward the same meaning, a persistent drift that reflects our cultural attitudes toward looking and feeling. "Sensory" is also possible, although it sounds a little harsh and refers more precisely to the internal physiological functions of sensing. It would be most direct, in English, to speak of the "sense" of the environment, that is, to its quality as sensed. But this adds a new meaning to many old ones. Even in noting that this is a new sense of the term, we reveal that confusion. We may also use a pleasant old word in a way now obsolete and declare that our subject is "seemliness," which refers to the qualities as sensed and also to a judgment that this quality is pleasing and well fitted to human capabilities. In some desperation, I shall use "sense" when I can do so without ambiguity, "sensory quality" when I must be formal (while lamenting its heavy tone), and "seemly" whenever that term does not appear too strange.

This essay, then, refers to what one can see, how it feels underfoot, the smell of the air, the sounds of bells and motorcycles, how patterns of these sensations make up the quality of places, and how that quality affects our immediate well-being, our actions, our feelings, and our understandings. The subject is broad. It ranges from the refreshment of shade on a hot day to the symbolic meaning of a sacred precinct. But it is far from all-inclusive, since it refers only to the direct effects of sensation, and primarily to the immediate ones. It does not embrace air pollution that is not apparent to an observer, however injurious it is to his health. Smog is a sensory phenomenon; carbon monoxide is not. The concept excludes many of the economic aspects of an environment, such as the relation of place to productivity or to cost, except as working conditions are directly affected by the sensory input. It excludes many of the long-range social or psychological impacts: the effects of the spatial separation of kin, for example, or of the nature of ownership.

But seemliness is not just a matter of esthetics. What is sensed has fundamental and pervasive effects on well-being. Esthetic effects are only a part of this total range, although potentially present in any act of perception. The esthetic experience is a specially heightened phase of sensation, different in degree, not in kind. Our concern includes the esthetic, but much more besides. The sensory quality of a place may be thought of as its most directly humane (or inhumane) aspect.

The sensed environment is a broad but definable and coherent subject. It is coherent in the sense (you see!) that similar considerations affect it, that it can be manipulated by common means, and that most people will see those connections as being reasonable. Since its central element is the interactive process of perception, its analysis must always include the perceptible features of an environment together with the capabilities, values, and situations of its perceivers. No useful conclusions can be drawn from a study confined to what is there to be seen or, on the other hand, from one limited to the way people see. Seers and seen must be considered together. We evaluate the quality of some particular sensed environment for a particular group of people.

This essay focuses on those sensory qualities of large, complex areas that can be most effectively managed at the scale of a city or a substantial urban district, a metropolitan region or a rural countryside. Urban and rural areas will not be separated here. They are part of the continuous spectrum of human habitats and are now becoming progressively more difficult to distinguish. This is the scale at which we live our lives today, the scale at which certain important sensory qualities are perceived and can most easily be influenced. But many other sensory phenomena vary by small locality, and all of them are sensed by single individuals in particular places. Our senses are local, while our experience is regional. So the discussion will cover things as large as air basins and freeway systems and as small as sidewalks, seats, and signs. Thus, readers may be confused as we oscillate between trees and forest. But developing rules for preserving specimen trees may be as strategic a regional action as zoning for extensive forest areas. I shall draw the boundary of discourse around the actions appropriate to the scale of management rather than around things of a certain size.

Who Manages It?

Many groups have a stake in environmental quality. They are not often those who actually create and manage it. The big builders, public and private, are not directly linked to the ultimate users but are only indirectly responsible to them, through sales or votes. The large private builder wants an appearance that will be attractive to the buyer at the moment of sale. The financier who stands behind him thinks of resale and is therefore pleased by conventional patterns. The public builder may be less conscious of the sense of what he makes, although his engineers are appreciative of order, simplicity, and an air of solidity. The public builder usually has the preoccupations of a manager: cost and long-term maintenance.

Both kinds of large builders press to get the job done—whether to make money or to get political support, but also because it is a matter of pride. They like forms that permit rapid decision, simple solutions, and clear demarcations of authority. They are pleased with solid, geometric, sharply bounded, smooth-surfaced things, set well apart. Public agencies, in particular, whose products are such a dominant part of our landscape, usually have few qualified designers on their staff. For these agencies, appearance is easier to think about if it is a final decoration—a bit of foundation planting, a commemorative statue, a handsome sign. Park boards have more explicit sensory goals, since their function is to maintain areas of natural appearance for the common enjoyment. Their model is the English park—the lawn with trees—a grateful form, but one monotonously repeated.

The drafters of zoning ordinances are also concerned with appearance (although they must not say so in a court of law). They hope for a pleasant and respectable setting, particularly in residential areas, but their aims are modest, in consonance with their instrument. They strive for homogeneity and order, precise zones, where everything can be found in its well-separated place. Drafters of building codes, on the other hand, have no conscious thought for looks, but their separate, simplified, technical requirements may result in some surprising sensory by-products. For example, the required roof parapet for firemen was for decades a principal generator of the city skyline, and the "two exits from every apartment" rule determines the shape of large apartment buildings today.

There are many other agents that shape the sensory environment. Individual owners change their home grounds to make them more livable and also to establish or to maintain their social position. Their room for action is limited. The manufacturers of environmental components—vehicles, street furniture, pavements, wall and roof materials, lights—think about the look of their product in a catalog but may leave even that aspect to a draftsman. They certainly cannot imagine how it will appear in actual use in the urban landscape. When they consider how the object will work, it is from the viewpoint of the manager who buys it, not the ultimate user. The managers of the public space, whose domain is daily threatened by accidents, rubbish, breakdown, and disorder, are quite naturally obsessed with surfaces that are easy to clean or to mow, stout forms, fences, warning signs, solid pavements, and that ubiquitous visibility and access which simplifies control. The sign companies and the individual merchants have their own sensory motives. They must compete for attention in the wilderness of form.

From the hands of these designers comes the physical world we live in. Even more, it is a by-product of other actions that take no account of sense at all: decisions on taxes, safety standards, interest rates, technical inventions, legal conventions, production processes, and many more. Our setting expresses them all, and, not surprisingly, that expression is erratic and often inhumane.

Governments that have broad responsibility for the welfare of all the people of an area carry out their responsibility by furnishing services, by regulation, subsidy, taxation, and other typically indirect means. It is not customary for them to manage sensory quality in any explicit way. Yet if their motive is the general welfare, they should then be concerned with seemliness. Many of their daily actions affect that quality—the construction of streets, utilities, and public buildings, the regulation of private builders, the taxation system, and the way in which they manage the extensive public space. I shall show that they have some additional means as well, should they decide to use them. But they will find little guidance from past experience for doing so.

Even in that bright future when all people control their own home ground, important regionwide tasks of sensory management will remain. These regional tasks are not confined to special areas and situations. They deal with continuous qualities—continuous over the area of the region and over the lives of its inhabitants. Sensuous qualities such as clear air or legible structure overflow local boundaries. There are physical facilities best provided by some one agency, such as main highways or large open spaces, or systems of things supplied from one source, such as streetlights, telephones, and directional signs. There are local areas whose users are so transient or complex that they cannot, or will not, take charge of them: a downtown street or a public square, for example. Regional agencies can provide a coordinating framework for local action and can equalize disparities in quality between different groups. They are able to collect, analyze, and disseminate sensory information as no others can. Regional sensory programs and workable solutions may be used by local groups, whether as a target or a reference.

Care for regional sensory quality should be the concern of regional government. Since there are few such governments in the United States today, my advice is aimed at the planning staffs of authorities controlling some large sector of a region—a city or county—and at those single-purpose agencies, such as highway authorities or metropolitan park boards, that are responsible for large parts of the environment and that arch across local governments. In an ideal sense, my recommendations would be most apt for the planning arm of a strong regional executive.

What For?

Why should any agency try to manage the sense of a place? What public purpose is involved, what social benefit? With a flourish of general phrases, most discussions of seemliness will take these questions for granted and so will plunge into the litany of problems and how to remove them, or an exposition of the methods of design and analysis, or a proposal for organizing the public effort. These discussions reveal enough confusion about the purpose of the whole endeavor to force us back to the starting point. Later, we can move on to methods and means. Working back from the nature of the final proposals, we usually find that public objectives have been reduced to an impoverished few: not to hear or not to see something that everyone agrees is obnoxious; or to preserve something existing that everyone agrees is splendid; or to get more trees and greenery. There is, however, far more to the task than that.

By describing purposes and giving examples, we also sketch out the possible content of a regional effort. By laying them out systematically—rather than by their priority or clarity or ease of achievement—we emphasize their grounding in the human condition. Specific purposes, priorities, and possibilities must be judged by local people in concrete situations. Therefore, these are *dimensions* of values, rather than explicit positions, but positions along these dimensions can be made explicit, as has been done in the imaginary examples worked out in Appendix 4.

The source of these dimensions is our current knowledge of environmental perception (see Appendix 3 and the Bibliography of Research), which is substantial, despite its numerous gaps and puzzles. This research begins to confirm that many requirements are quite general and others common to large groups of the population *(58, 76, 79, 100, 126, 132, 153, 163, 188, 195, 199)*. Clearly, there are as many that are idiosyncratic and that thus fall beyond the bounds of regional action. Some of this material is obvious, some exotic, but all of it is fundamental in its general form. Each time, purposes must be validated in the local situation. This essay outlines some of the dimensions of a regional effort rather than specifying rules for universal application.

Sensing and Acting

The basic test of a good sensory world is how effectively it supports the functioning of our bodies. The prime requirement is that people be able to use their senses: to smell, see, feel, and hear well. Sensation should be acute, informative, pleasant, and subject to receiver control *(65, 85, 117, 137, 170, 172)*.

Oppressive smog, monotonous noise, confusing displays, blocked views, and heavy odors are all restrictions on our sensing. Removing these restrictions is the precondition of all the purposes to be described. Special priority must be given to the sensory requirements of the handicapped, the visual needs of the deaf, the aural needs of the blind. Extreme sensory conditions—earsplitting noise, intense glare, prostrating heat—can prevent us from functioning or cause organic damage. Damage can be cumulative, even when conditions are below the threshold of attention. More often, sensory conditions disturb our comfort or reduce our efficiency *(95, 139, 144, 191)*. The disturbance varies to some degree with culture, the individual, and his role.

Nevertheless, generally acceptable standards of sensing can be set for particular types of areas and persons. They can be generated and validated by studies of preference and behavior. For example, the characteristics of outdoor noise (its energy level, pitch, and variability) are rather clearly related to the dissatisfactions and efficiency of the people exposed to them. Noise levels, brightness contrasts, or visibilities can be expressed in quantitative terms, while other attributes, such as the texture of light or the presence of socially embarrassing sound, must be described qualitatively. Still others that can be measured have yet to be connected directly to well-being. For instance, it is possible to measure quite exactly how large an object bulks in the visual field, but it remains to be shown whether this is a good predictor of dissatisfaction *(102)*.

The public purpose must go beyond removing the barriers to the senses and suppressing disagreeable sensations—that fixation on noxious odors, unpleasant views, or intrusive sounds which is the normal, primitive basis of public regulation. To bring the world within sensory reach, to increase the depth and fineness of our sensations, and to confer that immediate pleasure and well-being that come from vivid perception are more positive aims—not only to clear the air but to fill it with intricate things to watch, marvelous sounds to hear. Most people notice very little of what is audible or visible in their surroundings. They have learned to turn off their conscious attention. Our senses are biologically advanced and socially underemployed—they are consistently overqualified for their present use. Public management could put the senses back to work again, so that people might take delight in the luminous, odorous, sonorous world all about them.

Other organic functions are affected by the sensory environment: the motor actions of the body, and such fundamental interchanges with the environment as breathing, eating, eliminating, and maintaining body temperature and rhythm. There are substantial data, particularly in the extensive literature on ergonomics (95), on which definite standards for fitting the environment to these functions can be based, and these data can be confirmed by common sense and simple trial. Yet these considerations are routinely made light of.

What is worse, we completely forget the young, the old, the handicapped—everyone who is not "normal," healthy, and like ourselves. Places can be evaluated to see whether it is easy, or even possible, for the full range of users to perform such necessary tasks as climbing stairs, going through doors, crossing streets, carrying packages, and maneuvering a wheelchair (84). The character of the public floor surface, along with the control of its use, is a critical element in this regard. That floor is the literal ground of body action.

Urban landscapes, however, are not as single-functioned as the airplane cockpits or the machine tender's stations for which human performance standards were originally created. Behavior is variable and should be free to be so. Public places must be analyzed to see how they will support a full range of bodily actions, including those frequently encountered but not originally planned for: sitting on a stair, standing at a street corner, walking forward in a moving bus, running in a plaza, climbing a wall or leaning against it, sleeping in church. And are there places nearby where one can perform the universal functions: eat, drink, eliminate,

3 The stone seats that line Boston's Paul Revere Mall help to make it a warm
and sociable place.

4   In downtown Seattle, people sit on spikes or find a narrow shade.

bathe, and dress? Can one move about easily? The freedom to act is a valuable quality of the landscape. How often we see glaring misfits between places and what people are trying to do in them *(116)*!

Climatic conditions also have an important effect on the feeling of well-being. Heat and cold are the strongest body sensations, since they threaten the regulation of our internal temperature. Psychiatric emergencies have a significant correlation with weather conditions. Some environments protect us from climatic discomforts; others reinforce them. Most city microclimates are fountains of dissatisfaction *(147)*. We also maintain a stable body rhythm, as well as a stable temperature. Daily fluctuations of light, sound, and activity can support or upset that crucial internal pulsation.

Thus a whole set of environmental concerns cluster around the functioning of our bodies and of our senses in particular. The importance of these concerns is clear, however infrequently they may be attended to. For the most part, they can be converted into explicit criteria. A public agency could analyze a region in terms of any of these aims, set standards or guidelines for many of them, and program future modifications to satisfy them. A few examples, selected almost at random, will illustrate how many concrete issues there are, among which an agency might choose a few for serious study.

One could propose norms and standards for such things as
- the level and modulation of walkway lighting, its distinction from roadway lighting, and the lighting of hazardous places *(97)*;
- the minimum amounts of sunlight required in outdoor spaces;
- the frequency of outward views to be provided from public spaces *(21)*, and the conservation of panoramic vistas and of the access to them (see Appendix 4 for a more extended discussion);
- the prevention of reflected sunlight glare, and the encouragement of building surfaces that modulate strong light;
- a minimum allowable aerial visibility due to smog;

- a maximum allowable brightness and degree of motion to be allowed in signs;
- maximum sound levels for such purposes as preserving the ability to converse outdoors, to hear natural sounds, to allow sleep or study, or for the blind to orient themselves by hearing;
- the prevention of disagreeable or masking odors, fumes, and dust;
- the availability of places to sit and to lie down in public;
- the maximum allowable detours or delays that may be imposed on pedestrians before they can safely cross a street;
- a maximum allowable incidence of gross observable misfits between public behavior and environmental form (that is, those occasions when an outside observer can detect with certainty that a person is hampered by his setting—because he has obviously stumbled, is sitting uncomfortably, or whatever);
- ease of movement over public surfaces on foot, in a wheelchair, or on crutches;
- the paving, drainage, clearance, and cleaning of public walks;
- the availability of public toilets and baths, and their maintenance and supervision;
- public access to drinking water and to food;
- the provision of rain shelter, wind shelter, shade, outdoor cooling or heating, the prevention of wind tunneling or the dumping of heat into public spaces (see Appendix 4 for a more extended discussion);

and so on.

The agency might also

- analyze prevailing noise levels throughout the region;
- institute training-programs in environmental awareness;
- design prototype lighting systems (97);
- encourage the use of fountains, wind devices, heat and light sculptures, bells and music, decorative wall paintings, *son et lumière* shows, and other activities that extend and delight the senses (40, 170);

- recommend tax and regulatory policies conducive to clear air, or to the cleanliness of streets;
- propose systems of public arcades and shelters;
- make prototype designs of toilets, seating arrangements, and shelters;
- experiment with new paving materials, curbs, doors, and steps;
- test places for their fit with bodily performance;
- monitor the microclimate, its effect on the public, and how it is influenced by surrounding development;
- map the barriers to movement for the handicapped, or the degree of pedestrian detour and delay (see Fig. 42);

and so on.

Readers could surely extend these lists.

The Image of Place and Time

Cities are systems of access that pass through mosaics of territory. Access to places enables people to do what they set out to do. Territory, on the other hand, involves the spatial control of access and action, and man is a territorial animal. Territories range from the immediate bubble of personal space, through the home ground and the home range, to the domains of the largest social groups *(54, 83, 169, 180)*. Sensory factors interact with transport facilities and social norms, and so parts of a region are perceived as accessible or barred, open or closed, free or controlled (see Figs. 5 and 49).

A region can be analyzed to see if it seems accessible to its people—that is, whether they think that it is difficult to move in particular directions or at particular times, or that certain destinations are hard to reach or enter, and whether they are confused about how to navigate. On arrival, do people feel at ease in a place, so they can act normally? Only then is that place accessible. Thus a map of perceived access can be drawn for any given group. Social relations are crucial to this map, but so are the form and management of places. A "good" region, in this regard, has no large, con-

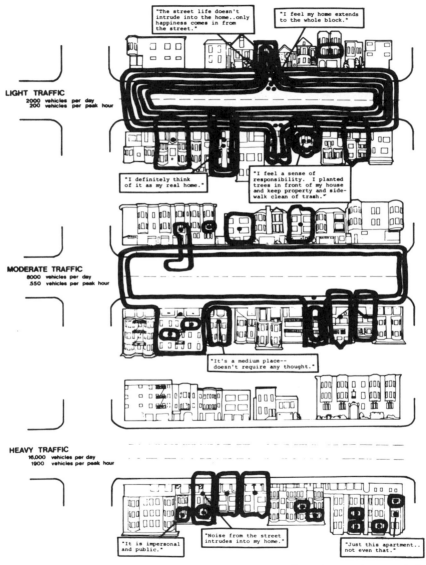

5 Local residents talk about their block in San Francisco and map their home ground.

tinuous areas of exclusion, and there are only small inequalities of access between different groups (see Fig. 6).

But while open access will penetrate this ideal region, most of its local places will still be defined and regulated to some degree. Much social behavior is territorial; that is, it is spatially defined and changes according to place. Territories are marked, defended, and controlled, and behavior is thereby stabilized *(54, 69, 176, 180)*. Some actions are proper to a territory; others are not. Effective behavior depends on the mutual recognition of boundaries and of the action that is proper to the place. There are transitions from one territory to another, and these transitional areas are often the most interesting places to be in, as any door leaner will testify. Thus a region can also be evaluated by finding out how clearly its territories are marked, whether the transitions are adequate, how finely the space is divided, whether the desired range of behavior is provided for, whether all social groups have territories of their own, and how well users understand and agree on the meanings and boundaries of those territories.

Access and territory are aspects of the mental image of space, considered as potential movement and action. But the identification of places, as well as their organization into mental structures, not only allows people to function effectively but is also a source of emotional security, pleasure and understanding. Orientation in space (and time) is the framework of cognition. We have powerful abilities for recognizing places and for integrating them into mental images, but the sensory form of those places can make that effort at understanding more or less difficult (see Fig. 48). So we take delight in physically distinctive, recognizable locales and attach our feelings and meanings to them *(74, 78, 81, 82, 90, 93, 111, 127, 128, 143, 176)*. They make us feel at home, grounded. Place character is often recalled with affection; its lack is a frequent subject of popular complaint. People are pleased to "know" a great city, or to understand its history. Indeed, a strong sense of

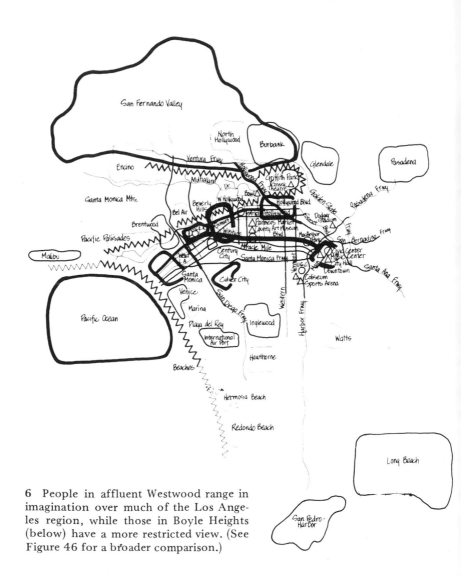

6 People in affluent Westwood range in
imagination over much of the Los Angeles region, while those in Boyle Heights
(below) have a more restricted view. (See
Figure 46 for a broader comparison.)

place supports our sense of personal identity. For that reason, familiar features of a landscape are often fiercely defended.

Professionals are frequently at a loss when dealing with these issues. They will make plans to preserve some physical aspect of a place, forgetting that identifiable character is a quality of interaction between observer and observed. The image held by the planner is blithely assumed to be the same one that is held by the inhabitant. Preservation of character is dwelt upon, but the creation of character, or the development of latent character, is passed over. Place character in everyday surroundings is hardly thought possible; it is considered to be a special concern reserved for unique or historic localities. Place identity and image structure at the regional scale are looked upon as esoteric matters. Yet for many people the region, or a large sector of it, is their true life space.

At the local scale, the issue is how well persons can define, and joyfully identify themselves with, the places in their home range (56): the home itself, the workplace, and the recreation ground (see Figs. 5 and 7). Identification derives not only from an interpretation of sensory quality but also from who controls the locale, who made it, how it is managed, and what meaning it has. A regional agency can only encourage those processes and institutions within which local place identity will grow. Yet a general diagnosis of the strength of local attachment is useful information. This very *localness* of place attachment serves as a warning against the indiscriminate application of regionwide standards of form. District rules should vary as places and people vary, and those rules should be developed and administered in conjunction with the local people.

There is a set of places whose identity concerns almost everyone. This is the true public domain—not the land formally owned by government, but those important exterior and interior spaces that are explicitly accessible to the general public and frequently used

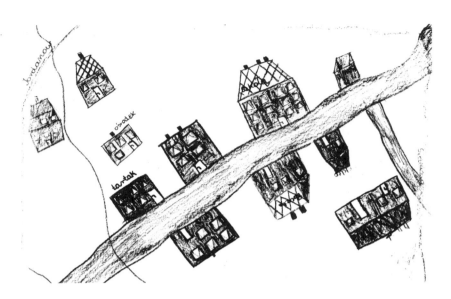

7 The home territory of a child in a Polish village: distinctive, secure, and bounded.

8 A twelfth-century map of Crusader Jerusalem imagines it as a cross within a circle, filled and surrounded by holy places. Compare it with the ancient Egyptian sign for a city.

by them—the main streets, the great parks and squares, but also the central lobbies, subway platforms, great halls, and department stores (see Fig. 15). The character of these elements, and their connection as a system, can be analyzed at the regional scale. One can evaluate the spatial form of such places (see Figs. 19 and 20), the experience of motion through them, their fit with the visible activity that fills them, and their images in the minds of users (see Fig. 50). The qualities of these public areas are subject to some degree of public influence.

Finally, at the largest scale, one may ask if the major elements of the region are clearly legible to most people: the main centers, routes, districts, and landmarks that structure the full extent of the area (see Figs. 8 and 46).

Certain types of territory seem to be almost universally essential to a satisfying landscape. For example, do individuals, or the smallest social units, have some place that they effectively control and can modify, where they may enjoy privacy? At mid-range, is there a home territory where they feel at ease, to which they belong both spatially and socially? At the other end of the spectrum, can they reach a place so removed from the concern of others that they can act there without conscious conformity to social demands? By this I mean those wastelands, wilderness areas, back alleys, vacant lots, hidden or empty places that are so useful as the locales for fantasy and free action, especially for growing children *(129)*. Private corner, home territory, wasteland—these should be available to everyone.

Although the spatial images of groups of people can be analyzed by a combination of subjective inquiry and field reconnaissance *(7)*, methods for analyzing the environmental image of time, which may be even more important to our emotional well-being than that of space, are unfortunately much less well developed. While the historic associations of certain special places are a common subject of planning attention, the usual aim is to save a few

old places just as they "used to be." How an entire working landscape might connect us to the present time, or to the recent past,
or to the future—indeed, to the unending *passage* of time—still
seems a remote question *(131).* Yet the lack of temporal connection in our landscape is a repeated and melancholy theme in literature. Moreover, there are temporal territories as well as spatial
ones: times of night that belong to teenagers, times of day when
market stalls occupy a plaza. Events and periods of time can have
character—or lack it—just as places do.

An analysis of the mental images that people hold of their life
space and life time is the key to understanding the sense of place.
Following from that understanding, regional policy can be directed to strengthening those images, whether by physical change,
activity regulation, institutional reform, or education.

Thinking of the sense of place and time, an agency might, for
example, develop norms for

- the degree to which inhabitants should feel able to reach and
  enter any part of the region that is larger than some specified
  size;
- the ability of children to explore their territory, or of the
  elderly or the handicapped to traverse the region;
- the perceived safety of being alone at any hour in various areas;
- the physical definition of social territory, and the preferred
  nature of the transitions between the public domain and group
  territory;
- the availability of orientation information, and the access to ex-
  planatory panoramas;
- the clarity of movement, connection, and approach that should
  be achieved along the major routes;
- the availability of wasteland;
- the imageability of public spaces, as well as more detailed rules
  such as the limits of their spatial proportions, or the preferred
  degree of enclosure;

- the limits on the height and bulk of structures that have neither a high degree of public meaning nor a high degree of public accessibility;

- the degree to which most people should be able to describe the spatial form of the region (just as we set norms for reading ability today);

- the degree to which an area should contain visual reminders of its past use and form (see Appendex 4 for a more extended discussion);

- the visible or audible communication of the time of day or season, of cyclic natural changes, or the schedule of public activities;

- the expression of current changes, future trends, and alternative futures;
and so on.
The agency could also

- create design guidelines calculated to increase the sense of place in new development;

- map areas to be conserved or changed, in order to enhance the sense of territory;

- analyze the legibility of the region and the sequential form of its main routes *(128)*;

- make a framework design for the structure of the region (see p. 43), and set up the sensory programs for areas and routes that would reinforce that design;

- map the degree to which the residents of various areas can change the shape of their home environments to fit their needs, or have already done so;

- study the underused areas of the region (rooftops, parking lots, tidal flats, back alleys) to see if they can be opened up to public use;

- propose a regional system of bikeways and footways, including their management and design;

- suggest how public access can be opened up to desirable areas such as waterfronts, nature preserves, streams, and fine viewpoints;
- develop prototype settings designed to increase environmental adaptability or openness;
- institute programs to train people in locating and using regional resources;
- encourage public celebrations of the seasons or special holidays *(131)*;
- develop information centers where current changes and future possibilities are displayed *(2)*;
- develop a plan for regionwide historic conservation, and set up programs of public education in regional history;
- suggest rules for moderating and redirecting the visible rate of change of the environment;
  and so on.

Landscapes and Communication

Any inhabited landscape is a medium of communication. Its messages may be explicit or implicit, simple or subtle. They may be displayed by persons or objects. The analysis of landscape as a communication medium extends far beyond the conventional exercises in sign control *(2)*. The multiple messages of the environment affect our performance, cognition, development, and emotional and esthetic satisfaction.

Information density—that is, the rate at which the observer receives information—is one critical issue. While driving, we may be overwhelmed with signals, many of them trivial or redundant. At other times, we are bored. Thus there is some (surely variable) optimum rate of reception, and in most public situations it is at least possible to identify the undesirable extremes. But even if this rate is within a suitable range, the information must also be legible: well-ordered, easy to read, congruent, and preferably rooted *(140)*. (By congruent, I mean that there should be a correspon-

dence between form and message. For example, an areawide prohibition should be expressed by marking the entire surface of the
area, while an exit sign is something that runs up to, and through,
the exit. By rooted, I mean that a message should be displayed at
the location to which it refers. Thus a beer sign would appear on a
tavern rather than on a highway billboard.)

All these dimensions of information—rate or density, legibility,
congruence, rootedness—can be evaluated without passing on the
content of the message, for content is a touchy issue. Most explicit
city signs are banal, and some are false. But censorship is an explo-
sive device. The urgency of certain messages—the public signs of
warning and control—can perhaps be generally agreed upon, and so
they can be given sensory priority. Otherwise, censorship is best
left to the individual. Make it possible for him to shut out unwant-
ed messages; he should not be forced to hear loudspeakers or to
watch blinking lights. From that point on, it may then be better
public policy to *add* valued information rather than to subtract it
by censorship. The messages that are most frequently wanted
should be there at hand: the time, the weather, traffic and parking
conditions, schedules and arrivals, activity identifications, the locations of public services, events to come, local news, and local history. Communications facilities in many modes should also be
publicly available: radios, telephones, mailboxes, television con-
soles, alarms, computer outlets, notice boards, newspapers. Yet
while some places should provide a feast of information, other
places are needed which, in contrast, are unusually calm and secluded, where one can attend to internal thoughts and sensations.
Indeed, to have access to a quiet garden in the very heart of a city
is a common pleasant fantasy.

The sensed landscape influences personal communication, as
well. It can set up barriers to meeting; its ambient noise can disturb normal speech. In contrast, there can be places where it is
natural and easy to meet and talk in small groups. There can be

larger places that are appropriate for the parades, celebrations, mass meetings, paseos, and promenades that are the essence of city life. The pattern of use and circulation itself may separate people or cause them to meet. The public domain may be visibly connected to a group territory in a way that invites an acquaintance. There can be comfortable niches at the edge of the action, where someone can unobtrusively watch that action or prepare himself to join it. The management of a place may make it easy for people to meet one another, or it can protect them against chance meetings. The control of communication is a central human activity (and, of course, a major source of political power).

The communicative environment is the ground for individual development. It stunts or drives that growth by the richness of the information it affords, the challenge of its contrasts, the room it gives for experiment and self-expression, the response it makes to any flowering. One important way of evaluating an urban landscape, therefore, is to see how it functions as a stimulus and a setting for education and self-development *(67, 72, 132, 134)*.

The regional analysis of the communicative environment is in part straightforward and in part problematic (for example, when one considers implicit messages, group variations, or the process of education). In some of its simpler aspects, its analysis and control will be widely accepted. Soon enough, however, one touches on warm issues of privilege and power. Yet these issues are crucial for the quality of the region.

Again, some examples of possible regional norms or guidelines for communication come to mind, dealing with such things as

- limits to the number of words (or other measures of information density) that are to be visible from any public location;
- the restriction of explicit visible information to that which is related to its site, except for specified purposes and in certain areas (see Appendix 4 for a more extended discussion);
- ways of ensuring the sensory priority of critical public communications;

9 Watching and acting,
children discover the
world around them.

- the prohibition of forced attention, except for critical messages;
- making available generally desired information (as determined by public inquiry);
- the location of information centers and of the various communication facilities that are to be accessible to the public (2);
- the availability of places to meet, sit, and talk in comfort, as well as places for large outdoor meetings, celebrations, and displays;
and so on.
In addition, the agency might
- map the density and nature of visible communications (see Fig. 43);
- design and operate prototype information centers;
- write ordinances controlling the sign system, and guidebooks for sign design;
- recommend the location and design of public signing;
- analyze how people receive and use environmental information;
- experiment with using the environment as an educational setting;
- enable small local groups to use the environment as a communications medium, while acting to prevent any dominant private control;
- recommend ways of providing public, secluded, low-stimulus places close to the areas of intense communications;
- create patterns for the form and management of places in which people may safely make new acquaintances;
and so on.

The Intuition of Life

The deepest meaning of any place is its sense of connection to human life and indeed to the whole web of living things. Many of the qualities noted previously contribute to this sense: for example, when a setting visibly supports biological and social functions, when it has a local identity and a clear temporal structure, or when it is rich in information. But a locality conveys that sense in other ways. Many of these ways are subtle and escape the awkward grasp of public action. Certain places seem cold; others vibrate with life.

The liveliness of a place is influenced by, among other more indefinable things, the transparency of the setting (that is, by how it makes visible the activity it contains); the way people can leave perceptible traces of their presence; the manner in which things express their action and purpose; the pattern of ownership, which always has sensory consequences; and the mix and density of movement and activity. On the other hand, how a place expresses the beliefs and values of its inhabitants is much more difficult to specify in concrete terms *(60, 78, 108, 109, 111, 118, 162, 184)*. One can look for explicit outward symbols or for the evidence of care and pride, but there is no analytical shortcut here: one must live in the place and talk at length with local people to uncover their deep associations *(7)*. It seems evident, however, that both the "liveliness" and the expression of values in a place increase as the degree of local control of that place increases.

We also delight in the presence of nonhuman life, in perceiving the natural context in which we have our being *(86)*. The regional analyst can record the visibility of animals and plants and of such elements as rock, earth, fire, water, and even the sky. Do smoke and banners celebrate the wind? Is information about the natural history of a place displayed? Is the natural cycle of seasons apparent? Can the rhythm of growth and of behavior be felt? Much of our dissatisfaction with cities can be traced to how they sensibly separate us from other people and from other living things.

To help correct this fault, an agency might develop norms dealing with such things as

• the desirable mix and intensity of activity in and bordering on the public domain;

- the transparency of the environment to the functional processes going on within it, and the presence of visible traces of human activity;
- the availability of seats and walks from which one can see activity and other people;
- the ability of groups and individuals to display symbols of their own values (as by permitting or encouraging street decorations, or the prominent location of symbolic community buildings);
- the frequency with which water, plants, rock, earth, and broad reaches of sky are to be visible;
- the preservation and enhancement of existing topography and ecology, or its visible recollection;
  and so on.
  It might also
- make prototype designs for increasing environmental transparency;
- encourage devices that will make one aware of natural elements and processes;
- design the settings and write the scores for public celebrations;
  and so on.

These four topics (sensing and acting; the image of place and time; landscapes and communication; and the intuition of life) embrace the basic reasons for planning and managing the sensory aspects of a region and lead to the relevant analysis and policy. However abstract they may appear in this summary, they can be linked directly to action. A regional agency may deal with all these aspects, since all are fundamental to human well-being. In Appendix 4, I have selected four items from the preceding lists of areas for action (maintaining distant views, providing public shelter, conserving local history, and encouraging rooted information) and have illustrated (though still hypothetically, alas) how these topics could be developed and what obstacles they might encounter.

While the value dimensions come from basic research, the emphases, criteria, and priorities arise from local time and place. They may be derived from more detailed, topical research (of the kind sketched in Appendix 3), or be forged by political conflict and consensus, or arise directly, as users participate in shaping their surroundings. I shall return later to some of these processes of setting criteria.

Our topics embrace vision and esthetics, but much more besides. They spring from ideas about how the well-being of persons and small groups arises as they directly interact with their settings, and not primarily from their role as passive observers. They encompass, in a more defined and operational form, the familiar terms of environmental improvement—amenity, appropriateness, uniqueness, harmony, preservation, naturalness, and so on—while centering explicitly on the human being. The more familiar concepts of environmental quality, so vigorously pressed today, are difficult to connect to basic human values or to carry forward to clear execution.

Planning for the sensuous form of a large area has usually foundered among vague descriptions. Our techniques should go beyond the lamentations, the "artist's conceptions," the exhortations, the overblown and unrealistic site plans that have up to now so often been relied upon. Based on concrete objectives such as those suggested earlier, policies may be written in explicit form, in ways that show how they would actually change future actions. The costs of these actions can be estimated, and the responsibility and timing for their accomplishment fixed. These plans can be translated into a public program and budget for sensory improvement. Elements that will be defined as substandard can be delineated. Modified drawings or photographs can show the predicted results, or a series of drawings can indicate a range of possible outcomes. Definite prototype and system designs can be drawn up. Specific sensuous programs, verbal and graphic, can be developed for selected places; "framework designs" can be made for the region. Later, these functions and instruments will be described in greater detail.

Context and Constraint

The world is not all will and purpose. A recital of aims may give an impression of limitless opportunity, but costs and limits are the other side of any coin that has values on one face. They will determine outcomes just as much as purposes do.

One general set of limits is the nature of the human organism as a biological and a social animal *(65)*. These human traits are built into the aims proposed and are their source. Other constraints are more variable.

The natural conditions of a region are an obvious ground and limit to its sensory form: its geology and topography, its climate, its ecologies (Figs. 37 and 40). Of course, topography can be modified by heavy machinery, and change in the microclimate is created by any settlement. Moreover, the ecological system is perforce reordered. But these changes have their costs, and the basic climate and geography of places remains relatively immutable, at least within our human scale of time. We are learning some sad lessons about the hidden costs of circumventing a site rather than adapting to it.

On this natural site there is usually a substantial framework of settlement, changing only slowly, conditioning all attempts to improve the sense of the region. Structures are in place, land is patterned and developed for use, the transport and utility systems are in operation. Thus urban regions are conservative systems with great inertia. Large-scale planning only manages and modifies the existing system; it does not replace it. In addition, there are nonphysical systems of the environment which are equally sluggish to change: patterns of ownership and of the control of use and development, communications networks and interrelations between localized activities, technological capabilities, widespread images and attitudes about environment, and common ways of using it. These patterns, directly linked to the spatial environment, must be understood if its sensory quality is to be managed. They not only set limits but help to define purposes and priorities as well. For example, an arid climate calls for shade and water, while private ownership of the land stimulates a search for public access to open space.

The limits set by culture and the political economy, as they have developed historically, are even more profound. The systems of production, consumption, and political power, the organization of the family, the relations between classes and sexes, and the values of the culture and the roles they permit people to play are basic conditions for sensing, since what is seen and what seeing means are social creations. These subjects are beyond the scope of this essay, however often their presence may be detected in these pages; but it must be obvious that they are at least as critical as the spatial conditions and are coequal with the biological nature of man in establishing the limits and context for environmental quality. Any analysis of this quality therefore begins with an understanding of the given landscape, its settlement, its history, its inhabitants, their culture, and their political economy.

The Administrative and Legal Context of Sense Management

From the outset, effective planning is tuned to doing something. A comprehensive survey of panoramic views is by itself unlikely to have any real outcome. It is more useful to consider which views the present zoning ordinance might allow to be blocked, since the ordinance can be revised. The more directly and independently any action can be carried through, and the better it fits with the existing motives of the doer, the better its chance of rapid success. A new planting plan for a park is more likely to succeed than a scheme that seeks to persuade the park board, the abutters, and the city to grant air rights for a café. To produce an immediate effect, one looks at the existing working agencies, their motives, their personnel, and their modes of operation and then tailors one's proposals to fit. Basic, long-term changes, on the other hand, require new institutions and new attitudes.

The legal basis for sensory regulation is changing, as the courts slowly slough off the peculiar notion that it is merely a matter of esthetics and that esthetics is a private, whimsical, unpredictable affair, quite distinct from such practical and "objective" issues as health, safety, and property value *(114)*. Health and safety turn out to be matters of judgment, too, since good health is actually not easy to define, and safety always includes some "reasonable" level of risk. Property value is often a reflection of sensory quality. Thus it is already legally justifiable to control appearances that cause a decline in property values if those appearances offend people and make them less willing to buy. But control is not justified if there is no property present that is susceptible to such loss and if only *people* are hurt. Strange! Moreover, some sensations are thought to be more "objectively" unpleasant than others. Disturbing noises or disgusting odors are obvious nuisances, subject to public control, while an ugly scene is a matter of taste and thus not a legal nuisance. (Visible nudity—if human, not animal—is an offense, however.) These anomalies are the residue of legal history, of lingering value hierarchies, and of common agreements in our culture. As such, they may be expected to respond to argument, experience, education, and changing values.

Yet the change is gradual, as is the nature of the law, and there are real (if blurred and retreating) limits to the public controls admissible on sensory grounds. Sensory requirements are therefore married to other concerns when presented for court test, or even cloaked by more "respectable" criteria. Rules against tree cutting are referred to ecology, or zoning setbacks are justified by the chimera of a future street widening. At the moment, the most common U.S. legal doctrine has shifted to the point where police power controls of sensory quality—as in a zoning ordinance—are permissible if "esthetic" reasons are associated with other reasons of health, safety, or property value and if they are not vague or left to the arbitrary judgment of some official. Sign control, for example, should, according to this doctrine, be justified by traffic safety as well as by informativeness or pleasant appearance. However, the close control of the visible form of buildings is allowable in a historic district, which is an unique "cultural resource" and brings in tourist dollars. Sensory control is still a parasite on other concerns and often relies on persuasion, incentive, and indirect effect. These limitations will be lifted only as sensory criteria become more explicit, more directly connected to clear public purposes, and more open to values that do not spring solely from the upper class or the professions.

Modes of Regional Action:
Diagnosis
Since any region is constantly being modified by thousands of private efforts, and most of them are only very partially under public control, how can a regional planning agency affect the sense of its region? One useful device in any pluralistic situation is *diagnosis*, since better information will in itself influence (and presumably improve) the actions of others. The agency may therefore analyze the quality of the region as it is used and imaged, issuing a periodic general report on the sensory state of the region and occasional reports on particular aspects. A diagnosis of the sensory state of the region will become the basic data for public action, for private development, for education, and for political agitation (see Fig. 53). It will also generate support for improving quality. One must acknowledge, however, the heavy costs of general surveys of this kind, as well as the difficulty of connecting them to action. They can be dustheaps of data, whose sifting absorbs the total energies of a staff. Thus analyses must be confined to a few fundamental conditions that will generate widespread political or educational

activity: noise levels, street cleanliness, images of use and access, or the location and rate of sensory change and by whom it is being caused. Otherwise, information is most useful when linked directly to some place or problem around which critical issues are arising. Timing and the mode of delivery are integral to its effectiveness. For example, a survey of the effect of existing tall buildings on public views will be hot news when height controls are debated, and an analysis of local territorial images will be timely when redevelopment is proposed. The diagnosis of a locality can be posted directly at that locality, so that local users can check its relevance. An analysis pertinent to members of some group should be delivered directly to them.

The agency may also examine the sensory results of certain completed projects, to see how they have carried out public purposes, as well as the aims of their perpetrators. Success and failure may be publicized. The practical usefulness of such checks must be obvious. Of course, they will lead to unpopularity with any builders whose inadequacies are exposed. The sensory consequences of proposed projects can be predicted, as a basis for regulation or decision. Proposals for major public works, such as redevelopment or transportation schemes, may be accompanied by predictions of their impact on noise, access, view, and so on. Private developers may be asked to make such predictions, subject to public checks; or, better, predictions may be made by agents whose interests are not at stake. In other words, sensory quality could become a normal element of the now-familiar environmental impact statement. But impact statements, so frequently required and so illogically paid for by the very people who pant for a positive answer, are now losing their effectiveness and becoming only an irritating delay in the development process. To prevent staff overload, lost time, and a massive production of "boiler plate," predictive requirements must be restricted to a very few critical projects, and the predicting should be done by a public agency not directly in-

volved. There can be even more positive returns if a regional survey staff will simply keep its eyes open for intriguing new structures, new uses, processes, and happenings that are just emerging
and that show promise of a broader application. Among the thousands of people who inhabit a place, astonishing things are always
being invented.

Policy

The agency would surely also develop sensory *policies* for public
adoption. These may be areawide performance standards or patterns, or they may be special norms for particular places and times
(see Figs. 10 and 11). Some of these policies can be expressed in
"framework designs," that is, designs specifying the general location and sensory character of desired regional features, purged
of all the physical detail that need not be fixed in advance (see
Fig. 12). Such a design may show that a future commercial center,
for example, is to be a pedestrian precinct of low, open structures
in a maze of narrow lanes, which contain a setting for neighborhood celebrations; that it is to be open to the sky yet sheltered,
directly connected to its residential surroundings, and yet visible
from specified points along the major routes of approach. Framework designs are highly abstract, flexible, large-scale site plans of a
kind appropriate to management at a regional scale. Such designs
call for definite public actions and place definite limits on private
development; yet they can accept many different specific forms.
Local groups may fill them out with more detailed programs. Designers engaged with particular sites can follow them with little
loss of creative scope. These framework designs would necessarily
be integrated with the more familiar land use and transportation
plans.

Changes in the design process may be recommended in regard to
user participation, public review, the way of choosing professionals, the use of competitions, the allocation of private budgets, the
sensory information that must accompany alternatives when deci-

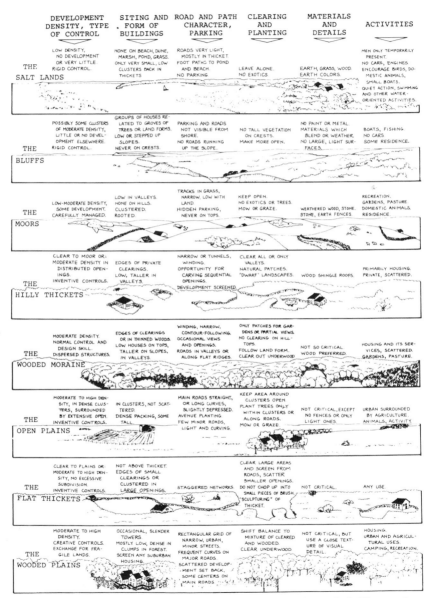

	DEVELOPMENT DENSITY, TYPE OF CONTROL	SITING AND FORM OF BUILDINGS	ROAD AND PATH CHARACTER, PARKING	CLEARING AND PLANTING	MATERIALS AND DETAILS	ACTIVITIES
THE SALT LANDS	LOW DENSITY, NO DEVELOPMENT OR VERY LITTLE. RIGID CONTROL.	NONE ON BEACH, DUNE, MARSH, POND, GRASS. ONLY VERY SMALL, LOW CLUSTERS BACK IN THICKETS.	ROADS VERY LIGHT, MOSTLY IN THICKET. FOOT PATHS TO POND AND BEACH. NO PARKING.	LEAVE ALONE. NO EXOTICS.	EARTH, GRASS, WOOD. EARTH COLORS.	MEN ONLY TEMPORARILY PRESENT. NO CARS, ENGINES. ENCOURAGE BIRDS, DO-MESTIC ANIMALS, SMALL BOATS. QUIET ACTION, SWIMMING AND OTHER WATER-ORIENTED ACTIVITIES.
THE BLUFFS	POSSIBLY SOME CLUSTERS OF MODERATE DENSITY, LITTLE OR NO DEVEL-OPMENT ELSEWHERE. RIGID CONTROL.	GROUPS OF HOUSES RE-LATED TO GROVES OF TREES OR LAND FORMS. LOW OR STEPPED UP SLOPES. NEVER ON CRESTS.	PARKING AND ROADS NOT VISIBLE FROM SHORE. NO ROADS RUNNING UP THE SLOPE.	NO TALL VEGETATION ON CRESTS. MAKE MORE OPEN.	NO PAINT OR METAL MATERIALS WHICH BLEND OR WEATHER. NO LARGE, LIGHT SUR-FACES.	BOATS, FISHING. SOME RESIDENCE.
THE MOORS	LOW-MODERATE DENSITY, SOME DEVELOPMENT. CAREFULLY MANAGED.	LOW IN VALLEYS. NONE ON HILLS. CLUSTERED. ROOTED.	TRACKS IN GRASS, NARROW, LOW WITH LAND. HIDDEN PARKING, NEVER ON TOPS.	KEEP OPEN. NO EXOTICS OR TREES. MOW OR GRAZE.	WEATHERED WOOD, STONE. STONE, EARTH FENCES.	RECREATION. GARDENS, PASTURE. DOMESTIC ANIMALS. RESIDENCE.
THE HILLY THICKETS	CLEAR TO MOOR OR: MODERATE DENSITY IN DISTRIBUTED OPEN-INGS. INVENTIVE CONTROLS.	EDGES OF PRIVATE CLEARINGS. LOW, TALLER IN VALLEYS.	NARROW OR TUNNELS, WINDING. OPPORTUNITY FOR CARVING SEQUENTIAL OPENINGS. DEVELOPMENT SCREENED.	CLEAR ALL OR ONLY VALLEYS. NATURAL PATCHES. "DWARF" LANDSCAPES.	WOOD SHINGLE ROOFS.	PRIMARILY HOUSING. PRIVATE, SCATTERED.
THE WOODED MORAINE	MODERATE DENSITY. NORMAL CONTROL AND DESIGN SKILL. DISPERSED STRUCTURES.	EDGES OF CLEARINGS OR IN THINNED WOODS. LOW HOUSES ON TOPS, TALLER ON SLOPES. IN VALLEYS.	WINDING, NARROW, CONTOUR-FOLLOWING. OCCASIONAL VIEWS AND OPENINGS. ROADS IN VALLEYS OR ALONG FLAT RIDGES.	ONLY PATCHES FOR GAR-DENS OR PARTIAL VIEWS. NO CLEARING ON HILL-TOPS. FOLLOW LAND FORM. CLEAR OUT UNDERWOOD.	NOT SO CRITICAL. WOOD PREFERRED.	HOUSING AND ITS SER-VICES, SCATTERED. GARDENS, PASTURE.
THE OPEN PLAINS	MODERATE TO HIGH DEN-SITY, IN DENSE CLUS-TERS, SURROUNDED BY EXTENSIVE OPEN. INVENTIVE CONTROLS.	IN CLUSTERS, NOT SCAT-TERED. DENSE PACKING, SOME TALL.	MAIN ROADS STRAIGHT, OR LONG CURVES, SLIGHTLY DEPRESSED. AVENUE PLANTING. FEW MINOR ROADS, LIGHT AND CURVING.	KEEP AREA AROUND CLUSTERS OPEN. PLANT TREES ONLY WITHIN CLUSTERS OR ALONG ROADS. MOW OR GRAZE.	NOT CRITICAL, EXCEPT NO FENCES OR ONLY LIGHT ONES.	URBAN SURROUNDED BY AGRICULTURE. ANIMALS, ACTIVITY.
THE FLAT THICKETS	CLEAR TO PLAINS OR: MODERATE TO HIGH DEN-SITY, NO EXCESSIVE SUBDIVISION. INVENTIVE CONTROLS.	NOT ABOVE THICKET. EDGES OF SMALL CLEARINGS OR CLUSTERED IN LARGE OPENINGS.	STAGGERED NETWORKS.	CLEAR LARGE AREAS AND SCREEN FROM ROADS, SCATTER SMALLER OPENINGS. DO NOT CHOP UP INTO SMALL PIECES OF BRUSH. "SCULPTURING" OF THICKET.	NOT CRITICAL.	ANY USE.
THE WOODED PLAINS	MODERATE TO HIGH DENSITY. CREATIVE CONTROLS. EXCHANGE FOR FRA-GILE LANDS.	OCCASIONAL, SLENDER TOWERS. MOSTLY LOW, DENSE IN CLUMPS IN FOREST. SCREEN ANY SUBURBAN HOUSING.	RECTANGULAR GRID OF NARROW, URBAN, MINOR STREETS. FREQUENT CURVES ON MAJOR ROADS. SCATTERED DEVELOP-MENT SET BACK. SOME CENTERS ON MAIN ROADS.	SHIFT BALANCE TO MIXTURE OF CLEARED AND WOODED. CLEAR UNDERWOOD.	NOT CRITICAL, BUT USE A CLOSE TEXT-URE OF VISUAL DETAIL.	HOUSING. URBAN AND AGRICUL-TURAL USES. CAMPING, RECREATION.

10 Guidelines for future development on the island of Martha's Vineyard are summarized graphically and verbally by landscape type.

11 A policy for controlling new buildings on the wooded ridges of Lausanne, Switzerland. Three dangers are to be avoided: continuous construction in front of the wood, interruptions of the wooded silhouette, or high buildings that peer over the wooded crown:

The proper solution is therefore:

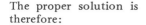
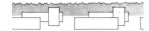

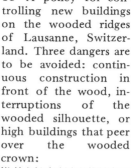

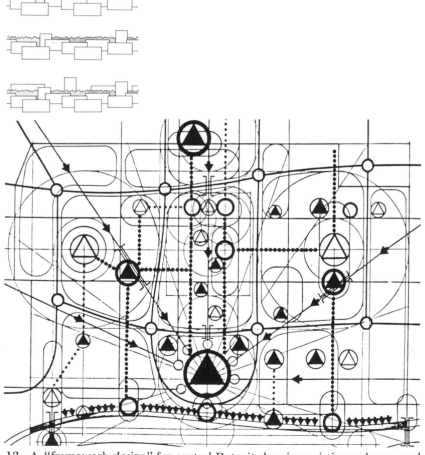

12 A "framework design" for central Detroit showing existing and proposed landmarks, visibilities, path gateways, foci, and visual districts.

sions are made, or a required conformance to programs that specify sensory performance. The rule that a certain percentage of a building's cost (typically 1 percent) be devoted to public art is a policy of this type, although it is a heavy-handed one that proliferates monumental sculptures largely ignored by the public. Requiring the reservation of a certain percentage of funds for subsequent improvements, to be made at the request of users after occupation, might be another, more effective policy.

Public policies dealing with management, financing, and taxation are more familiar to us and have substantial sensory effects. A change in the inheritance or property tax, for example, may encourage the retention of open space. Fees levied on certain effluents from manufacturing have been widely discussed as a way of moderating water and air pollution without resorting to rigid controls. Could fees also be applied to regulating noise, traffic generation, the blocking of sunlight, glare, sign size, and other measurable emissions? Or could ways be devised of granting market rights for sunlight, quietness, and so on, to local landowners and residents? For example, could one be required to purchase from a neighbor the right to cast a shadow on his building or his land? Incentives could also be outlined, to encourage desirable features. Policies would certainly include recommendations about public budgets as they affect sensory form.

Institutional shifts are yet another way of improving seemliness. These might include administrative changes that would put people with an interest in environmental quality closer to important points of decision or allow them a voice earlier in the decision process. A Public Conservator might be proposed and be charged with identifying and speaking for all those physical resources and qualities of a region which are of significant public value. New management and development institutions are frequently the key to achieving a new level of environmental quality. Homeowner associations, garden cooperatives, public development corporations, and integrated street authorities are just a few examples of such institutions.

Regulation

Keeping in mind the receding legal barriers, the agency would furthermore recommend *regulations* to control the sensory quality of private construction. Development regulations do not usually include explicit sensory objectives. But the familiar public controls—zoning, building codes, and subdivision rules—could deal with many things of that kind: the topographic siting of structures, their proportion, bulk, and visibility, their surface texture; the provision, proportions, and enclosure of open space; the preservation of fine settings, view lines (see Fig. 13), and sunlight access; the enhancement of natural features; the provision of seats, trees, shelter, toilets, and other amenities; the mix and transparency of street-front activity; pedestrian access and safety; the posting of information; and many more. Rules can be areawide or be tailored to specific locations. Most of these methods have already been tested in one or more real situations. In contrast to rules, bonuses—of density, use mix, height, or speed of approval—can be exchanged for public amenities, although there is a danger that the hidden public costs of the bonus may exceed the public benefits of the amenity *(3)*.

In a few highly significant locations, the agency may set out a detailed sensory program to guide proposals during design and to judge them during review. Design programs are normally confined to a list of gross physical features to be furnished: so many rooms, so many square feet of parking. However, programs would be more flexible and effective if they specified the performance wanted or, at least, if they outlined the general relations and qualities of the desired form. Sensory performance can be specified just as any other performance is specified. One can require a certain degree of visibility or of cleanliness, a floor traversable by wheelchairs, a level of spatial identity specified in terms of the probability of recognition, a degree of openness, the presence of visible nighttime activity, or the availability of certain information. More subtle qualities that are difficult to measure can be presented as "patterns" *(53)*—that is, as generic forms such as a recommended spatial relation between the car-parking area, house door, and private outdoor space; or how to provide marginal locations from which people can observe, but not quite engage in, some public activity—or as "analogues"—that is, by illustrative examples of other places that have the desired, but hard-to-define, character. Specifications for the preservation of environmental character are well known. Specifying a character to be created is more unusual and difficult. In fact, it is a new way of designing.

Projects that are in critical places or are critical by their own nature (for example, because of size, noisiness, or symbolic import) can be reviewed for their sensory impact. These reviews, based on public norms, programs, and framework designs, may be advisory or at times controlling. Design review is a flexible way of dealing with subtle questions of quality if the review is based on well-developed criteria and programs. But review has had an insignificant—at times even an adverse—influence when it has been administered by the usual combination of design professionals and developers, who, behind a screen of vague guidelines, pit profits against various ill-formulated design criteria ("harmony with neighborhood character," "human scale," and so on). Since review makes heavy administrative demands, it cannot be applied frequently. It will add to the uncertainties and lead times of developers. It is best applied during the course of the design, and not at some final make-or-break confrontation. With these warnings in mind, design review (coupled with a sampling of actual results) would very likely be a standard agency function. It would be even more useful if the review of some concrete proposal were also a review of the validity of the rules and programs by which the proposal was being judged. Innovative projects or unexpected consequences should inspire changes in law and policy.

Design

So far, except in reference to those peculiar abstract instruments called framework designs or to that unfamilar art of specifying future character by means of analogues, patterns, and performances, nothing has been said about *design* itself—the direct specification of form—the activity that most people automatically associate with a concern for sensory quality. The reason is that the ordinary design process is a dubious business at the regional scale. "Urban design" carries a dangerous germ of grandiosity: behind the concept of big architecture is a wish for big control. A hunger for the control of large-scale form is all the more dangerous because it coincides with strong contemporary trends toward large-scale investment. Big design requires substantial economic and political power plus a demanding technical effort to foresee and provide for everything. What is worse, it stifles local voice and initiative. The familiar result is a coarse-grained, inexpressive, maladapted habitat.

However, design can be used more judiciously, and this kind of design comprises a final bundle of functions for our agency. One such activity that it may engage in is "system design," that is, developing form and use possibilities for things supplied repetitively by public agencies: details such as pavings, fountains, fences, lights, or signs; features such as cycle paths, information centers, public corridors, light displays, or shelters; events and processes such as festivals, decorations, or even ways of piling snow; large elements such as prototype streets, transit stations, or pocket parks. System designs are concocted so as to be adaptable to local conditions by a rearrangement of parts, a choice of location, changes in dimensions, or the use of local materials or skills. These designs may be created in cooperation with a line agency or a manufacturer, or detailed performance specifications may be prepared for bid by suppliers.

A number of special design services can also be provided. Design handbooks may be prepared for public use. Prototypes of use and layout (a modest storefront, a small two-story apartment building, a backyard garden) can be drawn up for the general guidance of builders or residents who cannot afford to hire professionals. Private designers may well look on public design service as a threat to their livelihood. Yet there are so many occasions when design skill is simply not used, or is utterly subordinated to narrow private aims, that it is reasonable for a regional agency to use its staff, in this economical way, for public ends. A well-financed staff might go further, developing and testing experimental forms and ways of using them. Done properly, however, this is a long-term, costly, risky operation, crucial for the growth of our knowledge, but less likely to render immediate results.

Design services on special projects may be offered by the planning agency directly to public line agencies. The planning agency supplies its design skill, plus a knowledge of the present and future context of the area. In return, it receives a moderate fee and gains some modest influence over the outcome, although it does not make the decisions. More important, it learns something of the motives and limitations of the line agency. The feedback modifies the central planning; information flows both ways. Preferably, the loan of staff should encourage the line agency to build its own capability.

Design service can be institutionalized by assigning staff designers to particular areas of the region for service and liaison. In time, they become thoroughly familiar with a sector and its inhabitants and give the latter some leverage to modify the public and private decisions that continually descend on them. They would also be training local people to evaluate, design, and manage their own settings and might help them organize to exercise this control. Place character and populations are so variable that environmental quality is best tended in subordinate districts of the region, except where systems or issues concern the area as a whole. Clearly, the agency loses flexibility by making commitments for area design services, and they must be entered into cautiously. To reinforce any local commitment, a central agency would have some development funds of its own—small sums that could be parceled out to area groups for modest environmental or management improvements, on the recommendation of the local aide. The funds would be available to groups who had no other financial resources for the improvements and who were genuinely representative of the future users of that improvement. (Admittedly, both determinations are difficult!) The planning agency would not design, carry out, or manage the proposed change, although the design aide might furnish advice. The proposal would be reviewed on the basis of the explicit public criteria, how securely its future management was assured, and how well its proponents represented its future users.

An alert staff, choosing to focus on large-scale decisions, may use design service in still another way. It will intervene with suggestions, information, and criticism at the critical moment when key decisions are being made by others or when a conflict has erupted and must soon be resolved. This is the "brushfire" tactic. It requires diplomacy and the ability to respond within a deadline. It will not work unless the strategic moment can be recognized— the moment when decisions are not yet announced and not yet fixed but nevertheless will soon be made. The tactic necessarily ignores those builders, managers, and users who do not make dramatic decisions or who cannot make any decisions at all. All the same, this type of intervention, carried on by an alert and agile staff that has information at hand for a rapid response, can be an economical way of influencing sensed form, especially when development is proceeding rapidly.

Designing occurs in still another mode: "illustrative designs" show how an area might look and work if reshaped (see Fig. 14). Because they are not complete specifications and are not directed to any single decision maker, they can be produced with relative

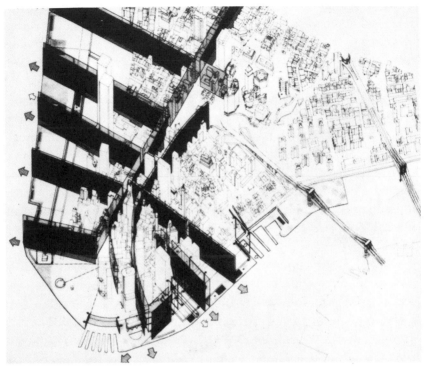

13 Visual easements, or "view corridors," to be kept open in any future development of lower Manhattan, shown here imposed on the existing buildings of the area.

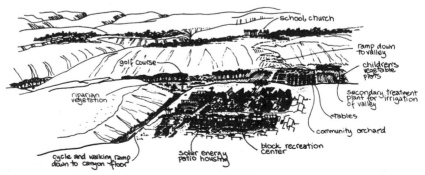

14 An illustrative design for San Diego, showing how its semiarid interior could be developed with tightly clustered communities on the flat tablelands and open spaces in the canyons below.

speed. They are actually public information about the possibilities of a place. Most professional designers dislike working on them, since they will never be built but will only dress the windows of some report. Indeed, they are often carelessly done, without reference to the real limitations and functions of a place, truly useless except to decorate a dull text. Even if carefully done, they will not be carried out as designed and so are likely to raise unjustified hopes and fears, despite the fact that they are explicitly labeled as illustrations. What is worse, they may be drawn to deceive, to "sell": the setting is altered; shapes are distorted or seen from impossible viewpoints; an unreal scene is filled with happy people doing improbable things. Despite these dangers, an illustrative design can transmit the intentions of a policy much more concretely than is otherwise possible. What a place might be is as useful a piece of information as what it is. With due caution, an agency uses illustrative designs to explore the meaning and consequences of the norms and regulations it is preparing, at least for internal use if for no other.

Direct attempts by the regional agency to control the detailed design of large areas or of the facilities managed by some other public agency will usually meet with disaster. In truth, public agencies are more resistant to public influence than most private builders are. The design of an area or system ought to be done by the agency that will ultimately be responsible for it, and its capability for doing this should be improved, not imposed upon. Occasionally, however, there may be some especially important public place that requires a coordinated design but is not managed by a single bureau. A gaggle of public agencies furnish and maintain parts of the place, and a multitude of private developers build the surrounding scene. A central planning agency may then attempt a "coordinate design," to integrate those public and private actions. This is a historic way of dealing with landmark locations. It requires a protracted effort, since the actors are many, often uninterested, and cannot be reached through any formal line of authority. Thus designs must restrict themselves to those features which are crucial to the quality of the place and must leave as many decisions as possible to the other groups. Coordinate designs become more like the sensory programs that were recommended earlier than they are like conventional site designs. Success hinges on good informal communication, personal skill, and on such levers as political connections, special legislation, or the money to buy cooperation. Given these advantages, a skillful designer can sometimes find a way to satisfy quite diverse interests; thus a coordinate design can be used to mediate a more general social conflict, or at least to initiate a process of mediation. A more effective, though also more protracted, method is to create a public or private organization that will have the power to build and manage the entire setting from the beginning: a street agency, or an association of owners. Environmental improvement depends on capable management institutions that are fitted to particular places and their users.

These four general functions—diagnosis, policy formulation, regulation, and the various forms of design service—make up the broad range of potential action for a regional agency. The relative importance of each function will shift with circumstances, according to the scale of the region, the level of its resources, the degree of consensus about environmental quality, and the centralization or decentralization of control. An agency with small resources, operating where controls are highly decentralized and consensus is lacking, might be expected to emphasize diagnosis, education, local design service, modifications in the design process, advisory reviews, the imposition of "effluent" fees, or the granting of market rights in quality. An agency with greater resources, operating under a strong central government and backed by a clear consensus, might rely more heavily on framework and system design, the design and management of public facilities, detailed regulations and sensory programs, taxation and incentives, and the creation of new environmental institutions.

Some of these varied means are familiar, others less so. Particular ones, new at least in this field, appear especially promising and cry out for trial and development. Included in this category are: the use of an area design service; changes in the typical design process to encourage sensory programming and user participation; the development of the sensory programming technique itself; the direct communication of local diagnoses; the public critique of completed, occupied, and managed projects; the imposition of fees or the granting of rights with regard to sensory qualities; better *management* of public space; and the creation of capable new environmental institutions.

A Strategy of Analysis and Action

A host of possible actions has been suggested. In a world of conflict and scarcity, one must choose a strategy of action. The key studies must be selected, arranged as a process within a time span, and fitted to the context of issues. One cannot deal with every question, and certainly not simultaneously. There are many levels and centers of regional decision, and studies are lengthy, decisions protracted. Rapid analysis and repeated consultation will shorten the feedback cycle; yet regional work is still painfully lumpy. Of necessity, the strategy is a succession of partial studies and actions, with a rhythmic cycling that is as long as two to three years. Gradually, this process deposits some understanding and confidence, an experienced staff, good or bad relations with other agencies, and a set of ongoing procedures (and ongoing red tape).

Most active programs did not begin by making a comprehensive analysis of the whole region, as might seem logical, but by carrying out a concrete investigation or design whose successful conclusion gave the planners the confidence and backing to proceed. They constructed their view of the whole as they moved from task to task. The delicate issue is how to initiate a strategy that will be self-reinforcing in the course of time and yet will not "harden," that is, one that can turn in new directions in the future.

The first problem to be dealt with may be one that is inescapable, since it was serious enough to precipitate the concern for regional quality. But where there is some latitude of choice, a problem is selected that leads naturally into other issues, gains useful allies, promises an effective solution, and furnishes some important general insight in the course of its analysis. These criteria may apply even to a study of the visibility of traffic lights, for example, whose successful treatment cements relations with the traffic department and leads to a consideration of the total system of communication in the street. On the other hand, a scheme for making parks out of existing vacant public land, if achievable, may gain a broader public recognition. An agency, like a person, learns by doing.

Most problems are presented poorly: either the solution is completely specified, or it is impossible. Untenable, hidden assumptions have often been made, and the implied values are dubious. Correctly stating the problem and negotiating that statement with the decision makers concerned will often take more time and skill than developing a solution. Typically, there is a desire to open up any problem: loosen its constraints, reach new clients, consider more basic objectives, widen the area of concern. For example, traffic lights contend with private signs, ignore the pedestrian, and are only one facet of a much larger problem of traffic management. Or to take the other example, is the vacant land better used for something other than parks? Yet this laudable, progressive widening of any issue, if followed to its limit, leads to the unanalyzable, insoluble Grand Question. Having first opened up the problem, later one is likely to be frantic to close it, as definite recommendations fall due. The negotiation and management of problems, with their rhythmic opening and closing, are made all the more difficult by the conventional long cycle of regional studies. Recommendations risk being reasonable answers to vanished problems.

Parallel difficulties arise in choosing the groups with whom to maintain liaison, since informal working relations are far more useful than those that can be maintained in massive progress meetings or through memorandums. Fortunately, the key regional agencies that affect sensed form, and even their key personnel, are likely to remain relatively stable over a period of years. How to build connections with local communities is much harder to answer. The necessity of local response has been a major theme of this essay, but it is rarely clear just who the community is or how it is changing. Local identity is the major source of permanent, effective concern for sensory quality. Thus a regional agency might choose to organize by local districts or to begin with local issues, reaching regional concerns at some later time (48). But this approach slights regional issues and capabilities, may arouse the ire of local government, and may commit the agency to a costly, permanent internal structure.

Maintaining community liaison will consume great-chunks of staff energy, especially in the beginning, before there is any mutual confidence. A hard-pressed staff will initiate community liaison only sparingly and gradually, remembering that lapsed participation is worse than none. The temptation of a well-sheltered staff is thus to avoid the issue entirely until forced by protest to attend to it. I argue that community liaison must be begun early but—as will be described later—that it can be highly selective and closely linked to the problem at hand and that such liaison groups can be progressively replaced. In any case, professionals are almost thankful for those major constraints—the topography, climate, and the general urban structure, for example—which are so dependably long-enduring.

Let us assume that some city or regional planning agency responsible to a capable government or coalition of governments (not a regional government in the United States, alas) and already engaged in the familiar realms of land use and transportation planning, economic and social analysis decides to plan for the sense of its area. Some immediate issue may well have pushed it to this point—air pollution, a sprouting of skyscrapers, a divisive freeway, or careless land subdivision. It has never done work like this before and will find little precedent in the literature. How may it proceed?

The agency first lays out its strategy: (1) a beginning phase that establishes skill and identity; (2) a mainstream of developing studies that are parallel or successive enterprises and whose emphasis can be shifted as the situation is clarified; and (3) some ensuing "steady state," where the sensory planning function becomes a normal part of the general planning function. Timing, budgets, staff requirements, problem statements, and political alliances must all be set out in this initial strategy.

In the Beginning

The opening phase needs some special identity. It needs new funds, and probably some new personnel. The usual bewildered response is to turn to consultants for an "urban design plan." This is unwise, since it is essential to build capability in the regional staff for the long pull (1). It is better to create a new internal section to tackle the main problem, while using consultants, if needed, to help lay out the campaign. Permanent staff will be required, with such skills as large-scale design, landscape evaluation, and behavioral analysis. But these specialists must be attuned to the peculiar difficulties of city and regional development. Some may be found within the agency; others must be brought in.

As with most programs that are new in substance and not yet commonly thought to be a normal government function, it is well to appoint a special advisory body, standing outside the existing political structure, which will focus on the issue. In this case it might be called a "Commission on Environmental Quality" and would be broadly representative of those groups which have a stake in that quality or which influence it: conservationists, developers and financiers, highway and utility engineers, artists and designers, open space managers, consumer and neighborhood groups, garden clubs, merchants, sign manufacturers, public health experts, newsmen, representatives of the elderly and the handicapped, and so on. A commission is a useful body. On the one hand, it can advise the planning agency and review its work; on the other, it can use its influence, exert leadership, and give weight and visibility to the issue. The balance of interests represented, the size of the membership, and especially the personal qualities and interests of the people involved will have an important bearing on that usefulness. But a vigorous commission will be a strong continuing force for environmental improvement.

The agency staff tackles the initial problem that has been posed to it without waiting for comprehensive data, but the analysis is so laid out that it begins to answer some more comprehensive questions and to open up other issues. Meanwhile, a rapid, general reconnaissance is also carried out—a superficial field survey backed with data from secondary sources and bolstered especially by discussions with a few knowledgeable people. It will look for quick answers to such questions as the following:

1. What is the basic spatial framework of the region: its typical areas, its principal centers, and major routes? What are the most striking sensory characteristics of these elements?
2. Who are the principal client groups with a stake in sensory quality at this scale?
3. What are the most obvious sensory problems and possibilities of the region?
4. What agencies and forces are principally engaged in shaping the sensed form, and with what apparent motives and results?

5. What are the probable means, within the agency's influence, which could change the sense of the region?

A more detailed plan of campaign can be drawn up from this survey, coupled with the experience being gained in confronting the problem originally presented. This plan would be reviewed with the commission.

Three Streams

Now the new program moves into the second, or development, phase, and it expands its operations. What follows is a rather comprehensive internal scheme that might be used by a large and well-staffed agency. Its exposition is not meant to suggest that this scheme is the ideal one but is intended only to display the possibilities among which choices can be made.

In this version, the work proceeds in three parallel "streams," each playing different roles and assuming different attitudes. Such a structuring of the task is intended to clarify and strengthen the essential aspects of sensory planning at an early stage. It is an interim structure. Information and personnel portage from stream to stream, and later these streams will mix or run dry. The first stream would be concerned with regionwide analysis and policy, in the traditional planning model. It would already have made the initial reconnaissance. The second stream is a new group that would work in direct communication with certain selected clients. The third would be a problem-oriented task force, which has already begun by tackling the original concrete problem. Continuing functions grow out of these three groups, but later they will be integrated into the general structure of the agency. A small special section concerned with environmental quality will be retained as a permanent feature, however.

The regional analysts of the first stream would complete the outline sensory analysis of the region: the identity, structure, and qualities of its major centers, paths, and districts; the variation in sound, climate, views, air and water quality, land cover and form;

the principal natural and historic and symbolic resources to be conserved. The principal question would be: How is the sensory form of this region changing?

While completing the field survey, this first stream would launch an image survey, that is, a study of how some general sample of the region's people use, conceive, and value their perceived surroundings. Subsequent surveys will reveal how that image is changing. The image survey is the correlate of the field survey and connects the internal landscape of the mind to the external landscape of the senses *(42, 55, 94, 128)*. It is also a convenient bridge between sensory phenomena and socioeconomic issues. Here we are at the source of values. Most sensory studies restrict themselves to a field survey: in doing so, they implicitly impose the professional values of their staff on the survey results, and lose much of the inner meaning of the sensed world.

Furthermore, this group would look at the way that decisions about environmental quality are presently being made in the region and how this process may be changing. Who decides, on what premises, and with what effect? Is this system likely to change? What would change it? What can the agency do? An early understanding of how things get done orients all the work to effective outcomes. The material from these three investigations could be the substance of the first report on the sense of the region.

On the basis of these three types of preliminary data, the regional stream or division begins to think about "what might be" at the regional scale. It roughs out some synthetic policies, constructs a tentative set of criteria, records some preliminary thoughts of what the regional elements might become. At this stage the group's thoughts will be far-ranging, even irresponsible. These are proposals made to be thrown away. But so design begins; without it, survey and dialogue are aimless. Concepts do not grow out of information, although it may stimulate their growth; concepts are tested by information. Too often, city design seeks only to conserve something or to ameliorate glaring problems. It fails to develop new possibilities.

While the first stream is working in this broad way, the second stream—let us call it the "root consultancy" since it will communicate with some of those who are at the "roots" of all the regional institutions—will move in quite a different direction. The general image survey will make some connection with people's needs, but the information so gained will be impersonal, remote, and aggregated. Moreover, it is not subject to reformulation by those who have been interviewed. The root consultants begin by selecting one client group, or a few groups, for an initial dialogue. These groups would be defined by an area of use or of habitation, or by class, age, sex, or ethnicity, or by their role in regard to the environment. Since only a few persons can be dealt with at one time, this will be a fatal choice. It might fall on the financiers of large real estate developments, the teenagers in a central ghetto, the homeowners in some new suburb, or the riders of a transit line. A group is chosen because it is especially powerful or especially disadvantaged or because it consists of people to whom the setting is particularly important. In any case, those chosen must be people whom one can hope to reach, from whom one can expect to learn, and who in turn can hope to have some environmental influence within reasonable time, if they do not already enjoy it. Regional politics and the critical decisions to come will guide that choice. Two important criteria of choice would be, first, that the group be central to some urgent regional problem and, second, that it be composed of people not yet heard from in regional decisions but who soon will or should find their voice. A group rising to political power or the occupants of a type of housing which is expected to overrun the region might be the ones first to be consulted.

Having made these first choices, the root consultancy would begin a dialogue with small samples of its chosen groups. The aim of the dialogue would be to help this set of people uncover their own images, attitudes, and ways of using places, their own problems and desires. The methods for beginning and sustaining such a dialogue have been developed recently *(71)*. If all goes well, these small groups will move to a discussion of what should be done and how it may be accomplished. The group may extend itself to include others of like interests or may decide to meet people with a different stake and thus to define agreements, conflicts, and accommodations. As the process gets under way, the professionals will shift to a reduced role—occasional technical support, liaison, or design services—and will eventually move on to talk with other clients. More and more of the action (if action ensues) will go on without them, and the issues will very likely move out into other realms than sense. In time, some individual professionals may choose to break off from the central agency, in order to play a consistent, permanent advocate role. Others may become official area design aides. But the root consultancy stream, as a unit, would not make a permanent commitment to any group, and this policy would be explicit from the start. The stream would periodically move on to other clients. It is engaged in design consultancy, not in advocacy. It aims to connect key groups to continuing environmental decisions and to liberate their environmental interests.

From the agency's viewpoint, this second stream is establishing sources of client information and trust which are far richer than can be gained by formal investigations. Its findings are not drawn from "scientific" samples but are derived from direct conversation. The activities of this stream may also create some political support (or alarm). At the same time, if new client organizations arise, they will begin to change the political atmosphere in which the agency operates. Thus the agency must maneuver carefully to prevent its capture by any single interest and to prevent its alienation from the government, which is the legitimate source of its role. Yet these dialogues should lead to some shift in environmental politics, or else they will be exercises in frustration.

The third stream of our hypothetical effort, the task force, has followed a different course. Instead of choosing sets of critical clients, it picks critical but workable problems: some public project that will be carried out in a finite time, such as the renewal of an area or the construction of a code of detailed environmental rules. This stream has already begun its first task and may take on one or two others if it has the capability. This is a conventional focused effort, made by a temporary task force whose composition depends on the nature of the problem. It would contain specialists other than environmental analysts and designers, but the problem would have been selected because it was important for sensory quality and because its solution hinged on environmental skill.

Task force involvement brings an immediate input of realism into the agency and builds support by demonstrating its ability to respond to urgent questions. The chosen project must have a realistic likelihood of success. The agency staff should be able to make a significant contribution to it and be able to learn from it. A magnificent, unrealized scheme (or a shoddy plan realized) will be fatal, especially as a first showing. The project must also be one from which the agency can break away, at some predictable point, since it will not want to be permanently involved in management.

Given this three-stream organization of the work, there will be problems of internal communication and dangers that roles and attitudes will crystallize. To caricature a possibility, there is a chance that "cool" technicians will gravitate to the first stream, "warm" community organizers to the second, and "hard" pragmatists to the third. Each group will be confirmed in its role and values unless information moves between the teams and unless personnel rotates. These are interim teams, not career sections. Here I have internalized points of view that are usually a matter of external conflict, if they are not dismissed entirely.

The emerging results of these three streams must be brought into relation with each other. The possibility of such adjustment must have been allowed for in the early choices of assignment. Tasks, clients, and analyses should converge on common issues. Now the general analysis of the first stream will be reoriented in relation to new client values or to previously hidden operational difficulties. New groups will be identified for dialogue with the root consultancy, or the consultants will be brought in to deal with the people affected by a task force problem. New problems, arising out of the original consultancies, will be set for the task force, or the way the task force tackles its problems will be challenged. Out of these interrelations, the three streams will make joint interim statements for wider review, first by the commission, and then by other agencies. The statements will include further reports on the state of the region, recommendations on policies, programs, criteria, and budgets, and proposals for reorganizing the process of managing sensory quality. The political and administrative reaction to these interim statements will cause the agency to carry out more definitive studies and designs. The relatively long cycle from regional analysis to regional action must be accounted for. Each study or act is designed to open the way to a successor, while steadily building a constituency. Education and action are always linked. Since the constituency for sensory quality may initially be weak, it can be argued that education should be emphasized, to begin with. But general education, not connected to live issues of action, will be dull and disengaging.

Any agency will naturally attend to those problems which seem most pressing and which it can most effectively influence. A large region may focus on air quality, landscape conservation, highway design, or the sensory implications of general settlement patterns. A small locality will look at litter, signing, landscaping, or ways of modifying the microclimate. A suburban area will be preoccupied with development control; a more remote region with tourist attraction; a center city with user management of existing housing, or the survival of its commercial center. An underdeveloped area will be absorbed by the sensory conditions for survival and health, while a more affluent society will be interested in leisure settings or in an advanced use of the environment for education and self-development. An area growing at great speed will want to know how to introduce minimum amenities into standardized construction, how to save valuable landmarks from destruction, or how to guide mass development so that residents will later be free to modify and enrich it. A declining area will try to find ways of retaining its people, of salvaging its heritage and turning that to new account. In some places, conservation and stability may be the big issues; in others, a preparation for environmental change, or the use of environment as a symbol for reinforcing social change.

The context of sensory planning will affect the methods used and the results obtained. One may be operating in a traditional, homogeneous society, with clearly articulated sensory values, or in a pluralistic and transitional one, where values are in conflict. Power may be firmly concentrated, so that the work is internal, technical, design-oriented, and aimed toward a few centers of decision. Or power may be highly decentralized. In that case, there will be greater emphasis on public information, education, programming, standards, and ways of opening up the decision process. All these variations in context cause corresponding variations in technical method. Moreover, problems and powers shift within a region, even if slowly, and the technical processes must be able to follow them.

The Steady State

As a steady state is achieved, the three streams will flow together or mix with other waters. The original effort will require a substantial staff, but the agency would be unwise to make this major commitment permanent. A large permanent section could mean a serious loss of flexibility and create still another set of impermeable professional boundaries. Much of the general analysis and policy preparation of the first stream rightly belongs in a general planning section, which would now presumably be aware of the sensory implications of its work and could absorb specialists in this area. Liaison with community groups is equally general, and its concerns overflow the bounds of sensory quality. A continuing linkage with user groups, accompanied by technical and design services to them, should be a normal function of any public planning agency. Similarly, task forces dealing with current urgent problems may be set up intermittently, their composition shifting as targets shift. From time to time, these may again be tasks where sensory quality is the prime concern.

Yet, while these functions are being integrated into the general staff, it is still important to retain a smaller specialized section. This will serve as the internal protagonist for sensory quality in situations where many issues strive for attention, and it can be the professional base for the environmental analysts and designers working in other sections. It will carry out special functions: conducting sensory diagnoses and evaluating sensory impacts; preparing design guidelines, programs, and handbooks; making illustrative, system, and prototype designs and patterns; and providing design services for community groups and other agencies. It will continue to act as staff for the commission. This permanent section should be small in relation to the total planning staff, which will always be involved in interrelated studies and must be ready to reorganize if new problems arise.

The agency cannot call this permanent section a "Division of Sensuous Form," which would be accurate, for North Americans would giggle at the name. "Urban Design Section" is the more usual term, although that implies that design is its only concern, that no one else designs, and that this section shapes the urban world. Moreover, it says that this group deals only with the city, and not with the countryside. Perhaps, then, it might be called an "Environmental Quality Section." This would correspond to the commission's title and would be especially apt if the team also dealt with matters of ecology, environmental health, and the psycho-logical and social impact of environmental form. This broad com-bination is certainly logical, although we have not pursued it here.

We hold no brief for the separation of sensed quality from other issues. Sensory issues must be forcefully represented in every plan-ning effort and must be considered on balance with the political, social, and economic implications of any public action. Planning for sensed form does not stand outside society.

Some Recurrent Issues:
Priorities

There are some familiar difficulties that arise in dealing with the sensed environment. One persistent question is the relative priority of sensory quality in relation to other environmental issues. More often than not, it is put low on the scale of urgency. It is thought to be a luxury, something one is happy to deal with when re-sources are plentiful. It will have high priority only where there exists some rare, endangered quality for which inhabitants have a strong affection, as may be found in some exceptional rural or his-toric areas, for example. But high political priority for such con-cerns is still unusual in the average U.S. city. Explicit sensory plan-ning has been done mostly in middle-class areas, affluent cities, or tourist regions. Policy makers still tend to agree with Thomas Jef-ferson in putting the "practical arts" first and the "decorative" ones later. Esthetics is often considered a kind of froth, difficult to analyze, easy to blow away. Our culture thinks of sensed form as a surface phenomenon, a luster applied after the inner essence of something is formed. But surfaces are connected to interiors. They play a key role in the functioning of the whole, since the surface is where any interchange goes on. All that we know and feel, beyond our genetic inheritance, comes to us from surfaces.

Concern with environmental sensation is not a specialty of wealth, although the sensory values of the wealthy may be more articulately expressed and more easily imposed on others. The sense of a place—its dust and its heat or the inhumanity it symbolizes—can be more important for someone who, because he is poor, is all the more exposed to it. The gaps between the environmental preferences of laymen and professionals, arising from differences of class as well as of training, have often been demonstrated. This discussion has indicated, not that environmental quality is unimportant to most people, but only that the criteria of quality differ or, more precisely, that while there are common dimensions of value, there are no universal solutions or priorities. Societies with few resources will spend a surprising proportion of them on symbolic sensory features: celebrations, cathedrals, fireworks, flowers, and colors. Survival is primary, but people will come very close to the edge of survival in order to satisfy their human ways of knowing and feeling. And survival itself depends on sensory function.

It is impossible to say in general whether sensory quality is an item of high, low, or medium priority. In every situation, some elements of sense will be crucial, others irrelevant, others of moderate importance. Whether the most relevant feature is the lack of shade in a brutal climate, the presence of a symbol of group identity, a clear orientation, peaceful surroundings, the expression of territory, or seductive textures depends entirely on the particular people and place. Environmental design is not a matter of marble, grand boulevards, and stately buildings. Some sensory changes are very inexpensive. Plain dirt and the weedy ailanthus are excellent sensuous materials.

Sensory quality is often dismissed in making public decisions because it is thought "subjective" and too variable for any common formulation in contrast to firmly founded standards of health, safety, and cost. Sensory quality is indeed subjective, since it deals with how people perceive and feel. But most standards of any importance are also subjective: the material goods thought necessary for comfort, the risk of death or accident believed reasonable, the

degree of mental stress that can be borne, and so on. It is because
these standards are so familiar, so explicitly codified, that they
seem "objective" and outside us. In fact, their specification is a
matter of value and subjective judgment and is based, as like as
not, on hidden assumptions. To some extent, standards rely on
judgments about all human beings; others refer to selected persons. No one survives decapitation; some survive tobacco. In the
same way, some sensory standards refer to the common human
animal; others refer to values and concepts peculiar to large social
groups; others are relevant to particular places or social roles or to
generic types of individuals; still others are hopelessly idiosyncratic. Public policy must be sensitive to these variations. But if it
is sensitive, then it need not—indeed, must not and does not—
shrink from questions of value and subjectivity. Let it be granted,
however, that sensory quality is subjective to its core, that it is
highly dependent on the particularities of places and people, and
that it is a subject not yet thoroughly explored. Therefore, sensory
policy will more often vary, from one situation to another, than
will other types of policy.

When perceptual quality is seen as a luxury, it may be the case
that regional effort has grown out of the personal convictions of a
few, rather than because of a widely expressed political demand.
The original resources for staff work will then be very scanty. The
study must move quickly from these first special interests toward
sensory factors relevant to issues generally perceived. Even the
"tightest" situations have sensory dimensions: the quality of daily
life in a squatter settlement, the sense conditions under which industrial labor is done, the effect of setting on the health and education of children. One begins with these immediate realities. But
issues of sensory quality usually have this very general tactical advantage: they affect everyone, they are apparent to everyone, and
they often seem (but only at first) to be less threatening to established interests than many other planning issues.

We can do without the lavish publications so often associated with "visual studies." Techniques can be rapid and simple. Volunteers can conduct field surveys and interviews, or untrained staff can be trained on the job. Expensive consultants may be used sparingly to help plan the process or to train local staff rather than to carry out the work. Luckily, the experiences under study are everyone's experiences, and the time lost in coordination and job training is well repaid in local interest and skill.

Conservation

Visual studies have been most successful when dealing with existing fine landscapes *(6, 9, 10, 16, 18, 19, 21, 34, 36, 41, 47, 49, 50, 51)*. Conservation is a relatively simple objective, and there will be political backing for efforts to save what is apparent to everyone. Unfortunately, most of our existing landscapes are incoherent, and in those places a beginning is more difficult. At first, there seems to be nothing worth saving. What might be is more intangible than what is, and there is more disagreement about it, since few can have experienced it elsewhere. Moreover, there is little hope that what might be will ever happen. So one begins where the local people are: How do they use the setting now? What are they doing to it? What features do they value in what may appear, to the outsider, to be a completely valueless setting? What discomforts are they subject to? What realistic changes might be made in a reasonable time? From small actions, set in local circumstances, one gathers the backing to move to wider action. Tangible achievements are powerful stimuli. Paint, plants, and signs can be useful beginnings, as long as first steps lead to further steps and do not chill our hopes as they visibly fade away.

Every region has assets worth conserving. It is unfortunate that people associate sensory planning only with rarity, wealth, and natural objects. Even landscapes that are well worth preserving can rarely be saved completely unchanged. Sensory quality is so interwoven with daily function, so dependent on contemporary perceptions of context and detail, that it shifts continuously. At most, conservative management is possible: guiding and restraining an evolving scene. It is the *rate* of sensible change, as well as its direction and its connection with past and future, that has the strongest impact on us. No place remains unchanged except heaven, hell, and outer space, and none of those is fit for human beings.

Sensed qualities are often connected to ecological factors, since many contemporary people find great pleasure in "natural" scenes, and since well-balanced ecologies normally have seemly appearances. The appearance of a place is usually a sensitive index of its ecological state, and care for the sensory environment can often be equated with the conservation of nature. This linkage to ecology has been a useful political alliance, but at times a befogging intellectual one. A good sensory environment is not made up solely of trees and rural scenes. Nor are all stable ecologies handsome.

Sensory quality is clearly related to the history of a place. Place character is the result of historical evolution, and thinking of how to conserve or enhance that character is illuminated by knowing how it came to be and what historic forces still sustain it. But the linkage of seemliness to history must not be taken to mean that concern for sensory quality is primarily an issue of historic conservation or that the evolution of places must never be abruptly deflected. Some history is irrelevant to the study of seemliness, either because it happened too long ago or because it is better forgotten. The fact that sensory quality has best been managed, up to now, in areas marked for preservation is a weakness in the field rather than a natural limitation.

Politics

The sense of place is also a political fact. What can be done to the look of a locality depends on who controls it. The appearance also reinforces the political pattern. People can be excluded, awed, confused, made acquiescent, or kept ignorant by what they see and hear. Symbols have great power. So the sense of the environment has always been a matter of moment to any ruling class, and rebels will break things up simply because they are symbolically abhorrent. But the sensed environment can also be used to protect a small community, to make life possible for marginal people, or to give symbolic support to a revolution. Elaborate, symbolic street decorations were often used in the early years of the Soviet Union, for example, and lighted candles in the windows heartened Danish resistance to the German occupation. Moreover, since many desirable sensory features are based on commonly shared human characteristics and are also what the economists call indivisible goods (a park system, clean air), it is as often true that changes in the sensory quality of the environment may improve the quality of life for everyone.

Nevertheless, sensory quality is a frequent factor in political conflict, although most often not an explicit one. Analyzing regional levels of quality makes clear how unequally sensory resources and opportunities are divided. Lots with fine views are more expensive and thus are occupied by the wealthy. Well-designed housing built for the working class is usually bought out by the middle class (Hampstead Garden Suburb is a classic example). This inequality plays a vital part in the debates about land and growth policy. As cities spread out, what is being sought by the new suburbanites is, in large measure, a better sensory environment, and what is being defended from invasion by their predecessors is the same. Understanding the nature of that quality exposes the injustice of the exclusion as well as what is threatened by the invasion. This knowledge could help us to ensure that the urbanization process, while increasing equality rather than decreasing it, does not at the same time obliterate the very thing sought after. As it is, successful improvement of environmental quality can all too easily magnify the inequality of enjoyment, except when it is an improvement of some public good or when it "filters down" over a long period.

Thus sensory studies may be suspect as being simply a cover for environmental domination. Sophisticated design has often been an argument for large-scale, high-capital development, and landscape conservation has sometimes been an excuse for excluding newcomers from some territory. An agency must be careful to reject this connection. It can do so by exposing the public consequences of some elegantly designed places. It can also seek to widen user control and so will favor work that deals directly with clients. The agency will accept a plurality of sensuous values and try to protect local spatial and temporal territories. By doing so, unfortunately, it can expect to lose some of its original constituency among leading social groups.

The locus of decision and control, the political question, is the issue here. Should environmental design be centralized or decentralized, and to what degree? Is it a field requiring such specialized judgments that goals and solutions must be set by skilled professionals? Do decisions belong in the hands of those who have the economic and political power, since only they can carry them out? The most familiar environmental designs require large resources and extensive coordination, and so their designers will readily take their places as the handymen of power.

Large-scale design has often been the means of solidifying or symbolizing centrality. Urban design had its origins in the creation of the earliest urban ceremonial centers: Teotihuacán, the great Mayan complexes, the cities of Shang China, the temple precincts of Mesopotamia and Egypt, and Chan-Chan in what is now Peru. The sacred awe induced by those monumental compositions was a direct instrument of the centralization of power in a redistributive society.

As an alternative, should we create what will sell, because the market is the best expression of popular desire? Or can one trust the democratic political process to balance competing demands? If so, one uses environmental design as a means of making conflicting demands and their consequences explicit in the heat of politics.

Other professionals will reject all these positions. For them, the correct line is to decentralize action as far as possible. Let everyone construct his own environment. Abolish the godlike designer, or convert him into a teacher among equals, a technical coworker. The professional mysteries of design should be transformed into information with which small groups can shape their own places.

This essay reflects the view that environmental control should be decentralized wherever possible but that decentralization cannot be absolute. Individuals, or least small groups, should be competent to make their own particular place if they choose to do so. Here the professional helps to create a widely diffused competence by teaching, by being a technical aide and a source of information, and by proposing possibilities. But there are important qualities that cannot be managed at a small scale—the shape of large open spaces or transport lines, systems of standardized objects, qualities of water and air, broad norms of socially acceptable performance. There are also many local places that cannot be assigned to any small, stable group of users. Intergroup conflicts must be dealt with, and the distribution of resources equalized. In these cases, the professional is a public technician, helping to manage the political process of decision and to keep it open and enlightened. Where clients are multiple, fugitive, or not yet present, he tries to fit places to the needs of those clients: as far as he can, he speaks for them. He recommends general policies that will convert systemwide decisions into local ones: general rules on user participation in design or on the scale and timing of investment. All this implies an emphasis on education rather than behavioral regulation, on action that develops widespread environmental sensitivity and skill, on openness and diversity of form rather than grand effect, on user control and user consultation, and on the use of techniques that keep decisions open and fluid. Clearly, this view narrows the possibilities of action, since many types of large-scale projects do not conform to these values.

Even within these contrasting attitudes toward centrality, there is another spectrum of belief that divides those professionals who accept things as they are—who, in order to be effective, put themselves as close as possible to where decisions are made today—from those who want to rebuild society, and so are concerned primarily with demonstration and political education. Each position uses its own set of analytic and design techniques. One cannot choose among these techniques on internal professional grounds. Political beliefs, one's model of man, directs the technical preference. But the technical choices must be made.

Environmental quality is often overridden by public and private agencies energized by profit, survival, or the drive to "get it done." Their single-minded devotion to these simple aims is their source of power but also the root of their neglect of seemliness. Very often, a planning agency must make concessions to these driving forces. It then seeks solutions and sensory criteria that do not threaten those primary aims. Bargains are struck, maneuvers are made in the cracks of the decision process, and so some useful work is done. A planning agency can raise issues, provide information, or facilitate political action. To go further, and to press for a transformation of the structure of society (which may well be what is needed) will be beyond the bounds of any official agency. True enough, its information and its way with its clients may help others headed that way.

The agency will have more modest choices before it. Will it work to serve (and slightly deflect) the groups now determining the form of the landscape; will it act primarily to check and contain them; or does it hope to modify the decision structure in some immediate, feasible way? Rebuilding the environmental decision-making process so that quality becomes an integral part of the internal measure of success for some agency is a difficult but lasting strategy. This third role is, in my view, the most important one. The "realities of development" (a euphemism for how things customarily get done at any given time) must certainly be well understood if an agency is to have any effect. But understanding does not imply abandoning the hope for structural change; on the contrary, it is a precondition for change.

Science and Sense

There are intellectual issues, not wholly separate from these political questions, which also surface repeatedly when one is concerned with environmental quality. Can we deal with sensory qualities rationally, or are they a matter of intuitive feeling? Do we need scientific evidence? Is it useful or possible to quantify sensuous data? What is the role of the artist or designer?

Once we take a position in favor of decentralization where it is possible and of democratic decision where it is not, it follows that we must depend on open and explicit methods. Goals, data, and solutions must be clearly stated and rationally connected, so that they may be openly debated. Artistic mystery is no more legitimate in setting sensory policy than it is in setting economic or social policy (although professionals in the latter fields create mysteries of their own). But intuition is not banished. It abides in the mysterious process of creation, which proposes the possibilities for public debate. It plays a crucial role in scientific discovery. Moreover, small-group decisions may continue to be intuitive or implicit ones, whenever such a group shapes its own place and so does not need to communicate its reasons to others. But public decisions must be systematic and open. "Matters of design" cannot be the last public stronghold of genius.

Scientific evidence of the connection between sensed form and human well-being is thus very valuable. It is not indispensable, however, or even always decisive. We do not need to establish eternal truth on every occasion. Scientific evidence is useful when it makes clearer to some user how he himself is affected by his surroundings or when it feeds those effects into a decision process that the user cannot otherwise reach. But, given an explicit decision process to which he is a party, he will often act correctly without scientific evidence. Scientific knowledge enlarges our grasp, but we already have some hold. We are all experienced in using our senses.

Moreover, evidence useful in this field need not mimic the form of scientific data in other fields. Quantitative information is useful because it is information in a more explicit mode, but it is dangerous to quantify phenomena that are elusive and subtle. Tightening up an analysis can open cracks through which meaning leaks away. The data most useful in environmental design are usually of the most direct, unprocessed kind: evocative drawings and verbal comments, movies of human actions, graphic records of places, poetic descriptions. Statistics are useful to record simple characteristics such as temperature, sound energy, the degree of visibility, use density, or gross explicit preferences. When elaborated to handle complex benefits, meanings, values, or characters, this numerical machinery will pulverize them.

Design is a confused word in environmental planning. It oscillates between two misconceptions: either that it is concerned solely with appearance or that it is a matter of planning buildings. On the contrary, design has a much more general meaning: it is the imaginative creation of possible form, together with a way of achieving it, that will carry out some human purpose. One designs a piece of sculpture, but also a gear or a seating of dinner guests. Design does not focus on appearance or, indeed, on any single factor affected by form.

The sense of an environment is only one consequence that flows from its structure—of how it was designed, if the form was deliberate. Occasionally, sensory quality is the dominant characteristic of a place, as in a pleasure garden, and occasionally it is of no account, as in a sewer layout or an automated warehouse. But wherever men are present and active, seemliness is at least one of the several significant consequences of environmental form. Along with those other factors, it must enter into the design of a place from the beginning. I have argued for a process of sensory planning that is closely linked to the daily decisions of public management and to all the other implications of spatial form. Its criteria should be operational and subject to test. Its workings should be political and open, attentive to the user, helping him to understand his relation to the landscape and making it increasingly possible for him to control it. This essay has tried to lay the technical groundwork for that political process. Is it necessary to add that technical skill, unaccompanied by social and economic change, will not produce the millennium?

Appendix 1: Work to Date

Examples in the United States

Comprehensive attempts to analyze the sensed form of cities and regions have been few in number—not many more than a dozen in the United States. The earliest was published less than a decade ago. We have much to learn from these first trials. No attempt will be made to summarize their content here; many of the urban studies are described by Michael and Susan Southworth in their article in the *Town Planning Review (46)*, and several analyses of regional landscapes are discussed by Peter Jacobs in the same journal *(18)*. In addition, a number of planning processes for managing sensed form at the city scale are compared by Irene Torrey in her paper on "Urban Design Mechanisms for San Antonio" *(48)*.

Detroit, Michigan, began a continuing effort in large-scale design for the inner city in 1963 and has continued steadily since that time, producing a string of reports beginning in 1969 *(13, 14)*. A recent report on the use and meaning of the central business district is a very interesting part of this series *(42)*. The design function is a permanent element of planning in Detroit and has had some influence on the built form of the inner city, working chiefly through advisory design review.

One of the first systematic sensory analyses was a visual analysis of the Town of Brookline, Massachusetts, made in 1964 *(24)*.

Many techniques were first tried out there. Today the most useful part of the report is the self-criticism of method in the appendix. The report had some influence in introducing a design review process in the zoning code, but little else. An early study of the visual form of Rye, New York, by Alan Melting, used many of the same techniques *(28)*.

Minneapolis, Minnesota, made the first large-scale comprehensive analysis of the form and image of an entire city, and this work has been published in a series of reports, beginning in 1965 *(29, 30)*. A later report examined the administrative problems involved in the urban design function *(4)*. These studies resulted in establishing a permanent Committee on the Urban Environment, a historic preservation committee, and the passage of state enabling legislation for special design districts. The studies gave further support to projects already under way, such as the Nicollet Mall and the system of second-level enclosed pedestrian ways. The planner responsible for the Minneapolis work is now carrying it forward in Dallas, Texas.

San Francisco, California, has recently completed the most thorough set of analyses to date, covering neighborhood quality, the street system, the general image, implementation, and objectives—published in a series of ten reports completed in 1971 *(43)*. The work culminated in a set of design principles that are to be used in reviewing new development. It resulted in the passage of a new ordinance to control building height and bulk and has furnished ammunition to numerous citizen groups seeking to conserve and improve the special features of the city. Environmental design is now a permanent function of the San Francisco planning department.

In other cities, such as Los Angeles, the design function was initiated by a comprehensive analysis, but it died out later *(23)*. The Los Angeles study had some interesting features, however, including an analysis of the image of some very different population groups and a series of concrete recommendations for public action. Other West Coast cities—Oakland, Portland, and Seattle *(33, 39, 45)*—did studies that were not long sustained. The Seattle reports, which had perhaps the briefest official life, developed some of the more innovative analyses, such as studies of parade routes, shadow patterns, and the timing of activity.

A statement of visual policy for San Francisco Bay and a recent study of the island landscape of Martha's Vineyard have shown that sensory aspects can be analyzed at truly regional scales *(34, 50)*. Both studies have had direct results in public action. The study of San Francisco Bay led to the important "design and appearance" component in the development controls now being imposed on the entire California coastline *(6)*. A reconnaisance of the environmental quality of the vast metropolitan county of San Diego has just been completed and distributed in tabloid form *(1)*. An analysis of the visual qualities of the Hawaiian Islands is an example of work at an even larger scale *(36)*.

Not all cities have chosen to attack these issues by means of a comprehensive analysis and plan. Some have opted to focus on influencing current decisions. Among these, one outstanding example was the work of the Boston Redevelopment Authority in the 1960s, which set high standards for the design of its renewal projects and took great care in choosing the designer it employed. Detailed design review was an important part of the process. The result was a series of individual developments of high quality. The level of quality played its part in the political support of the agency, which was under fire from other directions.

The urban design group attached to the Office of the Mayor of New York City and the subsequent offshoot of that design group to the staff of the Office of Lower Manhattan Development have operated partly through persuasion but primarily by means of zoning concessions given in return for the provision of plazas, arcades, pedestrian ways, visual openings, and other amenities *(3, 27)*. This group pioneered in the creation of special district regulations that make increases in density, or the ability to build on filled land, available to developers who provide specified features. The features to be provided are specially tailored to each area and written into the zoning code in detailed, concrete form. This policy has had a substantial impact on the speculatively "overheated" areas of the city, where density increases bear a direct relation to the profits of builders. It may also be leaving a legacy of rigid, detailed controls and hidden public costs.

In quite different circumstances, foresters, landscape architects, and park service professionals have been assessing the visual quality of extensive rural lands, as a consideration for rational management *(18, 19, 22, 38, 41, 44, 47, 49)*. Attempts have been made to classify scenery just as explicitly as woodland types are classified, to map visibilities precisely, to measure "uniqueness" as a guide to conservation (that is, if a thing is unique of its kind or within an area, how specialized is that kind, or how large is that area?), to scale landscape preferences, to use computers to predict visual changes, and to evaluate the visual impact of large public works in a quantitative mode. This work has continuing support and a direct outcome in forest, park, and rural region management. It does not deal with the more subtle elements of environmental quality, however.

A Few European Examples

The examples cited in the preceding section have been the most interesting efforts in this country up to the present time. There is another body of experience in Western Europe, with which I am much less familiar. A substantial study of the scenery along 43 miles of the Thames River in England was made in 1967 *(17)*. K.D. Fines classified the landscape types of East Sussex in 1968 and asked interviewees to rank typical photographs of these types by their "attractiveness" *(16)*. Maurice Cerasi followed some early experimental work in the Lodi region of Italy with a handsome analysis of the Ticino Valley near Milan, which integrates sensory, ecological, and functional analyses in a very evocative way *(8, 9)*. A detailed description of the center of Tenterden, in England, is a good example of the "picturesque" analytical methods of Gordon Cullen, prepared as a guide for the conservation and renovation of that town *(25)*. Arthur Kutcher has made a biting, graphic analysis of the relation of the Old City of Jerusalem to its visual setting, as a plea to stop its destruction *(21)*. Lausanne, Switzerland, has made a thorough visual analysis of its region, and its findings are being used in detailed development regulation *(10)*. Plans in the Stockholm region consider the usual form of the regional landscape, particularly as it is seen from the highways *(37)*. Plans for English motorways are now being systematically judged for their environmental effects, including noise, visual intrusion, the severance of access, and pedestrian exposure and delay *(112)*. These ill effects are reduced to specific measurements.

A Brief Critique

These studies have shown that analyses of quality can be made at the city and regional scale and can be brought to bear on public policy. They have also exposed some weaknesses, as might be expected. I mention some of them here, not as a blanket condemnation, but because they occur frequently enough to justify conscious correction.

The subject matter of these studies and guidelines is often unclear. There is a confusion of terms—amenity, design, esthetics, quality, vitality, and many more—all used in ambiguous and even contradictory ways. Surveys infrequently define what they are measuring or identifying in the field; instead, they often rely on vague common assumptions. There is great uncertainty about what the surveys should include. The Southworths found that 12 reports dealt with 96 different factors, ranging from soil bearing capacity to meaning, from pedestrian flow to citizen needs *(46)*. These factors were being judged by some 138 different criteria, from route clarity and the visibility of garage doors to architectural merit and the sense of excitement. Sometimes it is clear what is being observed or what the criterion of judgment is; more often it is not. Why one feature, and not another, is being recorded is rarely explained. Where do all these criteria come from? If some public concession is being granted for providing a particular feature, for what public reason is this feature wanted? Other recent work, yearning for respectability, builds numerically precise indexes out of multitudes of poorly defined and arbitrarily weighted observations.

There are often discontinuities in the information. A careful visual description will be followed by an evaluation that hardly refers to the items just described, because the evaluation results from feelings and principles distilled from other experience. The recommendations for action that follow may come from still another source, most likely a perception of what is usually done. That analyses are incomplete, crude, and at times unreliable might be expected in a new field, so meagerly supported. It is more serious that the analyses are discontinuous, or obscured with the camouflage of precision, or ill-adapted to the making of public decisions. Conversely, on the occasions in which sensuous quality has in fact been decisively influenced, we often find that the underlying information and criteria have been perilously scanty and inexplicit.

Despite the apparent range of topics, the studies have some noticeable limitations of subject matter. They emphasize vision over other senses. They speak for "normal" people, that is, for healthy, active, middle-class adults. There is little talk of the handicapped, the old, the children, or people of low income. The studies focus too much on special places—the plazas, the "untouched" rural scenery, and the great parks—with far less discussion of the broad areas of work and residence. "Esthetic" qualities are still being thought of as something separate from other aspects of living, whether esthetics refers to something decorative or something deeply spiritual. There is often a bias that favors natural settings rather than the man-made environment, except perhaps for the high-intensity urban center. The reports deal with a single point in time. They do not mention change, except in the sense of a past loss—or a threatened future loss—of some permanently valuable quality. Qualities and values and clients appear to be eternal. Divisions persist between those who favor a "process" or a "product" orientation in their work or between advocates of general policy and the believers in acting case by case. Few programs integrate these contrasting but inescapable twin aspects successfully.

These studies have been most eagerly and effectively applied in areas in which the fundamental task is to preserve *existing* qualities that are highly valued by articulate residents: historic districts, fine natural landscapes, well-to-do residential areas. Still another situation in which these studies have been warmly supported has been the central business district. But this also is a threatened area, in which improved quality will play a role in holding customers who are slipping away and where investors still have the resources to make improvements and the interest to motivate it. Important as the conservation area and the central business district have been as the forcing bed of sensory analysis, it must now go on to broader issues.

Sensory studies speak (or could speak) to very general fundamental human concerns. There is substantial, but still relatively inarticulate, political pressure to make use of them. They have far to go, however, to clarify their intellectual confusions and to become a working element in the process of city or regional management. Above all, they have yet to consider the experience of the landscape as it is enjoyed or suffered by the enormous variety of people who inhabit it.

Appendix 2: A Glossary of Technique

A list of techniques for describing, recording, and analyzing the sensed form of a large environment may be tedious, but it is useful. It cannot be exhaustive; new methods are always evolving. It will serve only as a rummage chest. We emphasize those graphic methods which are apt for specifying the pattern of some sensory feature in space and time. Some are well developed, others new and untried. The classifications used are simply for convenience in presentation; they are arbitrary and to some degree overlapping. Any agency would use only a few of these methods, depending on its purposes and capabilities. I have tried to indicate where each is most useful. Individual analysts and surveyors must be carefully trained and supervised to see that they produce comparable, reliable data. To do so is not easy in this field, where judgments can be explicit but are necessarily (and rightly) subjective.

Spatial Form
Spatial representations of some type are needed whenever the policy question involves reshaping the domain of public space. Scale models are a very natural and familiar way of representing these spaces. Normal models are useful at moderate scales, but they are rather illegible and extremely expensive when large areas are being studied. While they impress the public, they will absorb much

energy, and they are difficult to revise. One is easily deceived by diminutive scale and the view from above. Some device that projects one's vision into the model should be employed: a mirror, a viewing tube, or a tiny camera. Movies may also be taken in a model to give the illusion of passing through, but the lack of detail and activity can be deceptive (see p. 97 and Fig. 29).

Models are frequently used to urge some big scheme on a bewildered public. They are more honestly used as an accurate representation of an existing context, into which alternative versions of some new development can be inserted for evaluation (for the effects on scale, silhouette, visibility, the relation to topography or to existing buildings, and so on). Some European cities maintain a permanent model of the center as a means of testing all new proposals. A model may also be the medium in which the design for some public space is developed, being patched and modified as ideas grow. For this purpose, simple cardboard or clay models are best, since they can be more speedily prepared and changed.

One may deliberately distort the scale of a model, or certain features of it, to emphasize something: magnify vertical distances, differentiate new buildings, make doorways stand out, convey a mood. A "negative" model is sometimes used to describe spatial form when the space is interior and complex. In this case, solid objects are ignored, and the empty space is modeled in some transparent material as though it were a solid form. Diagrammatic models are also possible. In these, spaces are represented and located by solid abstract symbols whose color, shape, and size convey the general importance and spatial character of each place: its scale, enclosure, activity, and so forth. These three-dimensional diagrams are particularly useful for studying regional systems of space and can be made quickly.

A whole series of two-dimensional graphic techniques have been developed to describe spatial patterns. The simple coverage map is useful at a moderate scale (see Fig. 15). It may be supplemented by an indication of building heights and an indication of the principal interior spaces. In this way, one acquires a sense of the entire system of public spaces and can judge their relative capacities, linkages, and sequential form (see Fig. 16).

Long sections can be cut through a square, along a street, or even through a city sector, if it has a decided topography (see Fig. 17). Isometric bird's-eye views are very legible if there is little masking of one feature by another (see Fig. 18). But they are tedious to make. The old technique of laying building elevations out flat along the edges of streets and squares as if they had been squashed onto the map is a childlike, telling way of describing spatial form (see Fig. 5). It is most useful where street lines are occupied continuously, but it cannot deal with interior space. And it gets into trouble at the corners.

One may record whether the public spaces have good proportion and scale, clarity of form, and a degree of enclosure *(61, 66)*. Some of their critical sensory characteristics (their sound, for example, or their light, or their relation to human activity, or their textures) still escape precise graphic or verbal description. Nevertheless, one may analyze and record more general judgments. Do their light, sound, and texture seem to reinforce their character? Do their elements have a size and a prominence that befits their public importance, or does the city hall crouch beneath the insurance building? Is there a good fit between the visible human activity in a space and its size, shape, and equipment? How well are these spaces interconnected visually and functionally? Can people move from one to another without hesitation? Are the entrances to buildings and other private domains clearly identified? Realistic drawings may be supplemented or replaced by diagrams that symbolize some of these selected qualities (see Figs. 19, 20, 21). A simple map diagram may express the degree to which various spaces are accessible to the public. Another diagram may express the relative scale and degree of definition of each space and how it is linked to other spaces. Still another may indicate how a place is "filled" with its activity, sound, and light. Spatial diagrams (or diagrammatic models) present information in a very condensed way. They are quickly made and very useful for staff analysis. But one must be careful that the scaling of these abstract dimensions ("degree of definition," "activity fill," and so on) is explicit so that the findings could be replicated by any trained observer. Unless the legends are extremely clear and the abstract dimensions connect with known issues or experiences, they may puzzle a public audience.

Rather than making a precise recording of the three-dimensional system of public space, a regional study engaged in a broad diagnosis may convey the normal scenery of an area in a set of typical views. Photographs are quickly made and familiar to read. They hold a wealth of detail, including the evidence of ongoing activity. Everyone believes them to be truth itself, but of course they can be as deceptive as any drawing. In addition, they lack selection and are difficult to reproduce. Recent studies indicate that people can extract more information from undistorted drawings than they can from photographs (167). For clarity and expressiveness, for ease of reproduction, and above all for the way it forces an investigator to *look*, nothing approaches the simple, undistorted, freehand sketch, made on the spot and perhaps corrected with additional photographic evidence.

Since there is no limit to individual scenes, one must decide which ones to portray. The natural method is the one used to illustrate guidebooks and tales of travel: one portrays those few locales which seem to epitomize the range of scenery that comes to mind when one tries to remember the setting (downtown, slum, outer residential suburb, historic center, abandoned farm, and so on). In skillful hands, this is evocative and economical, but its source is personal bias (143). Has some important type been neglected? Is the classification illusory and cross-grain to reality? Does it give a balanced picture?

More systematically, one may identify the typical sublandscapes and then map the entire region into them, seeing that no area is neglected and that the classifications are definable and reasonably distinct from each other (see Figs. 22, 23, 24). The typology is successively amended until one has what seems to be a satisfactory mapping of the region, with a description and views of each type *(50, 122)*. The typology should have some fit with other kinds of data, and in particular it should have some meaning for public action. Thus one may end up with a map that in effect locates areas that are substandard in seemliness or which require different treatments if they are to be developed properly. The basis is still subjective. The analyst runs the risk of creating a district where no one else would see one and the equal risk of burying some important distinction. It is difficult to settle on the edges of such districts, which in reality blend into one another. Moreover, if the quality of one district depends on adjoining ones—as when the views out into other places are important—then the method gets sticky. But at least the classification is explicit and comprehensive. Whenever it is desirable to vary a policy according to the area to which it is applied—when making rules for siting buildings according to topographic form, for example, or when weighting conservation decisions according to landscape rarity—then this type of analysis may be required.

Another, more objective, technique is based on some regular sample. For example, an even grid is superimposed on a scale map of the region, and a representative photograph (or drawing or panorama) is then taken at each grid point or as near to that point as can be reached (see Fig. 25). The fineness or coarseness of the grid is a matter of judgment, depending on the resources available to do the job and an estimate of how frequently the sensed landscape varies. One now has an orderly sampling of the region, which as a whole conveys the balance and nature of typical settings and in detail can furnish a view close to any point desired. A mapped typology of the previous kind can be prepared from this sampling, but the data remain and permit a remapping based on a revised typology. The views at grid points can be supplemented by symbols or brief written descriptions. This data base on the sensory landscape can be stored and called up at will. The cost is relatively low, since the work is mechanical and the equipment simple. Photogrids of similar scale allow the comparison of different regions or establish a record of how a region is changing over time. They can be presented singly, or successively to give a general impression, or can be pasted on a gridded map. The photogrid is a basic record of very general usefulness. Naturally, before an agency undertakes such a generalized recording, especially before it commits itself to a regular updating of that record, it considers whether the cost is justified in comparison with the piecemeal acquisition of new information each time a new problem arises.

In place of studying large spaces or landscapes, the analyst may choose to look in detail at some of the typical smaller clusters of spaces, objects, and activities that are repetitively encountered in the region. Thus he may record a typical row house and its yard, a typical block of ribbon commercial frontage, a street corner, an elevated station, or a schoolyard. These are the building blocks of the landscape; they correspond to the "behavior settings" described later, and at this scale spatial form can be described together with behavior patterns. The study of settings will be particularly important when the agency is analyzing the relation between behavior and form or is evaluating some particular project, or if it is preparing to do prototype designs. In this case, the techniques used are the usual architectural ones, supplemented by the behavioral diagrams described under the heading "Spatial Behavior."

Temporal Form

Historical maps and views are usually relevant to a regional analysis. Even better is a series of maps, or of sketches or photos taken

from some unchanging viewpoint, which convey the sequence of
development. Changing maps, models, and views can then be vividly presented as time-lapse motion pictures, but such sequences are
costly to prepare. Special maps may differentiate areas or buildings according to their age of construction or last major recon-
struction. Since these maps demand a careful survey, they are justified only when some concrete renewal or preservation plan is
being considered. Maps showing historic and architectural features
of special interest, presumably those to be preserved, are often
used (see Fig. 26). This is a description that fits directly into policy decisions. Selection is usually a matter of expert judgment,
which it is assumed that everyone will accept, and may be made to
seem objective by using composite rating systems. This objectivity
is misleading, since histories and values differ among different people. It might be more accurate to show areas or features historically relevant to particular groups or interests.

Maps could be made of the density and nature of the signs of
time in a region. These would include references to the past that
are noticeable to a knowledgeable person: historic buildings, ruins,
inscriptions, monuments, graveyards, old trees, traditional activities, and the like. They would also include places where the time
of day or season can be read, and where there are perceptible signs
of coming events: preparatory activity, visible trends, the communication of future intentions, and so on. Such a map would be
a basis for improving the public communication of time *(131)*.
Surveys of this kind have yet to be made. Up to now, concern
about temporal form has focused entirely on historic preservation.

The general rhythm of use and appearance may also be dia-
grammed: the 24-hour locations, the business-day places, the holiday places, or those which exhibit other regular cyclical changes in
appearance (see Fig. 27). A staff may do this either because it is
thinking of making a more continuous use of the public space or
because it wants to encourage the concentration of activities that

coincide in time. A mapping of the cycles of activity may reveal marked inefficiencies, disharmonies, or conflicts in the temporal occupation of space. A more subjective mapping could be made of localities that have apparent tempos that are "fast" (nervous, rushing) or "slow" (quiet, placid).

Change may be analyzed by way of maps that display three linked factors: the rate of present environmental change as it is distributed over the region; the locus of future change that can be reliably expected (because of strong irreversible trends or plans already going forward); and the places where there is some explicit conflict over the future environment. These characteristics of change could be compared to the public visibility of change, if that had been mapped as described earlier, in order to reveal the discrepancies between appearance and the underlying reality. Again, one cannot cite contemporary examples of this kind of analysis. But it would be an excellent way of summarizing one aspect of the landscape that is crucial for policy and also for how people feel. Many unseen changes in the landscape, which by their invisible approach generate such anxiety, can in fact be made quite apparent. Hopes, simple possibilities, and even conflicting plans can be displayed. A planned building can be staked out, the land to be taken for a highway can be outlined on the ground, or two alternatives for future use can be demonstrated directly on the site.

Sequences

People experience a large region as they journey through it *(37, 57, 185, 190)*. A planning staff must deal with that experience in some form, yet the problem is to reduce the analysis to some manageable scale. For that reason, a whole vocabulary for describing the sequential experience is developing.

The traditional way of expressing a sequence is to couple a base plan with a series of slides or sketches taken from successive viewpoints (see Fig. 28). With a camera, this is simple to do and easy to understand, especially when one is making a presentation to large groups of people *(143)*. Showing the views, one after the other, is a surprisingly good substitute for the moving view itself. But slides confine us to the visual experience and, within that, to a narrow angle of view, unless side views are shown concurrently, a cumbersome procedure. They are not precise descriptions. The selection should certainly not be biased toward a single mode of travel if several are possible along the path. The bus rider or cyclist will see things differently. Too many photographs or drawings are needed for sequences at an extended scale or to allow the analysis of a whole network of sequences. But a photographic series can illustrate typical segments, within a more general, abstract mapping. One can also imagine an elaborate storage system that would allow one to call up successive views in any part of a network in either direction. New views could be inserted in the record as the real setting changed. One might even use the sequences to test the visual result of inserting some new structure along the way. But this requires delicate photomontage work on a whole succession of views. Sequential drawings can also be used to illustrate a new design, but the work is laborious.

Motion pictures are an obvious extension of this method, since they are successive views presented so rapidly that the eye reads them as real motion. Movies are easy to take from a vehicle but more difficult to use for simulating other modes of travel. Although they are the natural medium for presenting motion, they suffer from some of the same limitations that affect a series of views: visual emphasis (although a sound track can be added), a narrow view angle, dependence on the selective choice of the photographer, the bulkiness of the data (even worse than in the slide sequence, since movies occur in real time), and an inadaptability for showing new proposals. Movies are expensive and slow to prepare besides, although videotape avoids this particular difficulty. Single photographic sequences are simpler to use and often more effective.

The motion picture technique can be employed in various modifications. It is possible to make movies of sequences through models that are reasonable simulations of the real thing (Fig. 29), although expensive equipment is needed to make them properly. In this case, new proposals can be illustrated, modified, and compared with existing conditions. Another device is the time-lapse movie, in which the moving view is caught, frame by frame, at extended intervals. The result is a motion picture that simulates passage at frightening speed. But after an initial perceptual adjustment, the viewer can read the general form of a long sequence from this high-speed presentation. At the same time, he has a collection of single frames, taken at regular intervals, for detailed study when he needs them. Since time-lapse movies are easy to make, they are a good way of gathering comprehensive base data on an entire system of major sequences in a region. Indeed, they are the sequential analogue of the photogrid described earlier and have the same general usefulness. They are less useful for public presentation, however, except for their shock value.

"Cartoon" movies can also be made to describe some new sequence, if a sufficient number of drawings are made; but this is obviously a tedious exercise. The old-fashioned "flip cards" are a much simpler device: a succession of quickly made drawings or photos, which are stacked so that they can be riffled through rapidly. The effect is surprisingly realistic. In sum, motion pictures are effective presentations, but—except in the time-lapse form—are expensive and not easily usable at more than a local scale.

Because of these cumbersome difficulties, several languages have been created for symbolizing the elements of a sequential experience in a single two-dimensional drawing. The elements to be represented may include changes in view, space, apparent motion, light, sound, activity, and many other factors. One must learn to read such drawings; but once the language is mastered, a sequential experience can be imagined from them, much as music can be read from a score. These languages range from simple to complex, impressionistic to precise. The impressionistic but flexible scheme used by Appleyard, Lynch, and Myer *(57)* was one of the first of these (see Fig. 30). The technique created by Philip Thiel *(182)*, and still developing, is the most sophisticated and thorough (see Fig. 31). From these diagrams one can read details, analyze separate factors, or attend to the whole experience. They are easy to manipulate; they can be used directly in design. But at first they look mysterious. They demand some training and are therefore not very useful for public presentation.

Sequence diagrams can be reduced to very simple, selective notations. For example, one may represent only the sense of entry—the "gateways"—plus the visible approaches to dominant features. Or one may symbolize only the relative clarity of direction along the routes, plus the legibility of each principal decision point *(43)*. And so on. These diagrams are economical analyses and now are usable in public discussions.

Visibility

General views are sometimes an important feature of a regional landscape. There are some simple ways of analyzing what can be seen at a distance. The principal viewing points of a region can be identified, and the angle and depth of the possible views from each point can be shown on a map. This diagram can be supplemented by panoramic photographs or sketches that show what can be seen (see Fig. 32). The reverse technique is to locate on a map, in some simplified form, the essence of the distant view of each prominent feature that is seen repeatedly from many locations: a skyline, a large land or building mass, a key landmark, and so on (see Figs. 33 and 34). These analyses are relevant whenever the conservation or creation of panoramas and landmarks is likely to be an issue.

Having a library of the significant views of a city makes it possible to apply scaled drawings or model photographs of new buildings to them and thus to test the visual impact of those buildings. Given such a drawing, the general public will see this future impact in a very direct and convincing way.

More systematically, one may map the total extent of ground that can be seen from some one critical location, noting in addition those features most prominent in that field of view (see Fig. 35). Of course, this is also a mapping of the areas from which that location is visible. This may be done for all the commanding locations in a region (all the hilltops, for example, or all the viewpoints accessible to the public). Maps can show the areas from which a particular class of feature is visible. Thus one delineates the parts of an island from which the sea can be seen, or the streets along which at least one tall landmark is visible, or the places where one can catch a glimpse of the open fields surrounding a town (see Fig. 37). Isolated visual compartments can also be defined; these areas can be treated as independent units because one cannot see out of them and they are invisible from the outside (see Fig. 36). Or areas can be scaled according to their powers of "visual absorption," that is, the degree to which they can absorb new development without marked visible change, because of their irregular topography, heavy plant cover, or the coarse scale and diverse mix of existing development. Systematic coverage of these various kinds is required as one contemplates general policies, such as to prevent new development from intruding into a view, or to increase the visibility of open fields or the sea, or to minimize the rate of visible disruption.

A "visual corridor" is the same representation done from a pathway and is an essential step in studying the potentials of the view from a road (19, 22). In this case, a route and the envelope of possible views from it are shown—the total extent of ground that can be seen while traversing the route in one or both directions.

Within that envelope, the prominent features may be picked out: hills, landmarks, water, building masses, panoramas. This is a simple way of defining the visual impact of a landscape as seen from a single path. The visibility field can often be delineated from a good topographic map (see Fig. 38) and then checked in the field *(123)*. There are computer programs that will produce such maps, once the topography has been fed in. View analyses are particularly important whenever the issue is new development on untouched ground.

Symbolizing the visual connections between major features is a more abstract way of showing the same data. The symbol for each feature is linked to every other feature from which it can be seen. Transferring this network to a scaleless topological diagram of visual linkage is a further abstraction. This may be done for particular kinds of features, such as public spaces or main roads, that are visible one from another, and the diagram would be used in analyzing the structure of a regional system of elements.

"Visual intrusion," measured in millisteradians (a precise measure of the spherical "surface" of the field of vision of an observer, at a particular location looking in a particular direction, which is covered by some particular object), can be calculated for critical locations and objects, such as an expressway, the sky, trees in general, or a large building *(102)*. This number can be tabulated, mapped at points, or even shown as a field of varying "intrusiveness" lying about the object or distributed over a region. A protractor has been devised to allow the rapid calculation of this measure from plans. Finally, it is possible to record the general conditions for sight. For example, light intensities can be mapped at night, to show where vision is possible or easy. Visible smog or haze can be recorded for typical (or worst or best) conditions, by shadings or isograms that describe the maximum extent of clear vision at a given location and time.

Ambient Qualities

Much of the sensed quality of a place resides in its climate, particularly in its microclimates. There are well-developed techniques for describing these phenomena *(147)*: wind roses, isotherms, combined indexes of temperature and humidity, the intensity of rain and snow, cloud and fog patterns, and so on (see Fig. 39). Gathering these detailed data will be difficult, since they rarely exist for urban areas. (In the long run, a detailed survey may well be justified.) For want of better data, one turns to impressionistic mappings: locations that seem particularly hot or cold, where there are wind tunnels or wind reflectors, places where sunlight glare is annoying, and so on. Locations in which the public can shelter from rain or wind or sun can be noted. Shadow maps show the areas that are in shade for varying percentages of a sunlit day (see Fig. 40). They are relatively easy to prepare, even for large areas, given the latitude, a good map, and the vertical dimensions of things. All these data lead to an analysis of the climatic problems of a region and point toward ways of ameliorating them. Thus the localities that lack public shelters or suffer from excessive glare or wind would be identified as targets for public action.

Excessive noise is a common city complaint. The energy level of prevailing noise can be mapped for various typical times and the measurements adjusted for pitch to match the acuities of the human ear. This has been done, on a sample basis, even for large cities. A simpler, more graphic, version will reduce this quantitative survey to various degrees of effect on function or well-being: Where is the noise level painful or organically damaging? Where does it mask other sounds? Where does it repeatedly interrupt normal speech? Where does it disturb sleep or study? Where is one consciously aware of it? Where can one hear delicate sounds, such as the rustle of a leaf? Where does it seem deathly silent?

Noise level should not be the sole focus of policy. Southworth has shown that it is possible to map the quality of sound *(172)* as well as its intensity (see Fig. 41). Sound can vary by intensity, pitch, and the mixture of these factors over a duration of time (which can be recorded on a sonogram—a small, reproducible graphic record from which a sound can be reconstructed and by which a trained reader can identify it). Sound is further complicated by reverberation and spatial configuration, and it has such subjective dimensions as apparent loudness, brilliance, deadness, rhythm and melody, warmth, and information content. Echoes inform us of the size of a space and the nature of its boundaries; objects cast sound shadows; people and activity broadcast their presence; a place makes its audible response to us. It may be useful to characterize key sounds in this way or to describe the aural form of particular places. But this task is normally too detailed for a regional analysis. Again, sound quality might be simplified to a mapping of the audible field of selected desirable or undesirable sounds (church bells, music, birdsong, early morning garbage cans, helicopters, jackhammers, and so on).

The quality of daylight and nightlight is an important factor in the sense of a place—it can be characteristic of a region, especially in certain seasons, or peculiar to parts of a region. It is often alluded to but rarely analyzed. Nor is it easy to analyze in any direct or mechanical way.

The artificial lights of the city are among its more intriguing aspects. One can record something of their quality in photographs and study their pulsation through the night in time-lapse movies. Light contrasts, textures, colors, or sources can be mapped for different areas in a quantitative way. One can describe how well light is fitted to functional requirements or to what degree it expresses the presence and activity of people (think of that ghoulish sense of a totally illuminated yet empty office building versus the small lighted windows of an inhabited house, for example). The investigation depends on what public guidance of lighting is contemplated. If the only intention is to suppress glare, then the analysis is straightforward (but it should include daylight glare, as well as artificial glare at night). Standards can be set for acceptable ranges of light intensity, for the degree of light contrast, for the rate of pulsation, or for the location of lighting in relation to the requirements of use and the clarification of the environmental image. Designs may be made for modulating public lighting, for illuminating landmarks, or even for creating new luminous landmarks.

Smell is a suppressed issue. It is rarely discussed except when some noxious odor is to be eliminated. The word itself is pejorative ("this place smells"). Yet smell is an intimate part of the character of a locale: smells of the sea, of hay, of fat frying, of bread baking, of wood smoke, of the crowd. Smells evoke memories; they can be delightful or abhorrent. There are informative, spatially orienting odors, such as the scent of a flower or of beer from a tavern. There are masking odors, which blind our noses by blanketing other smells, as when products are made to smell "fresh" or when automobile fumes pervade the streets. Particular odors can be described quite precisely and analyzed sufficiently well to reproduce them. But the description of their spatial range, their mix, and their temporal variation has not yet been mastered. However, if the public aim is simply to control unpleasant phenomena, the detectable range of such strong or masking odors can be mapped. Methods of design for introducing odor sources to the landscape or for guiding the siting of developments to take advantage of odor sources are still unborn.

Details and Surfaces

"Street furniture" is worth looking at if an agency intends to design some system of these objects or to recommend the control of their location, as in sign control or the coordination of light and utility poles. The list of details is very long, however: waste receptacles, doorways, cornices, drinking fountains, curbs, public toilets, shelters, arcades, newsstands, and so on and on. The public landscape is made up of endless combinations of these things. Which ones are worth analysis depends on which really have a strong impact on perceptual quality and at the same time can be managed successfully. "Visual studies" have often concentrated heavily on these public details, because they are objects that can be designed as designers are trained to design. But certain details will usually have a greater importance for the man in the street: toilets, doors, signs, arcades, and lights are likely to be particularly significant for human activity *(174)*.   •

One may be concerned with the general nature of building facades and thus may map such things as color, overall texture, the prevalent surfacing material (brick, shingle, stone, stucco, clapboard), the normal ratio of the area of openings to closed wall surface, or the typical surface modulation (flat and smooth, or deeply pierced, or with frequent swelling bays). In some cases, the silhouettes, or even the surfaces, of the roofs may be an important part of the scene. Studies of building texture are particularly useful in areas of moderate size recommended for conservation or whenever it is important to fit new development into an old fabric.

The "floor" of a city—the public ground surface, indoors and out—is always one of its more important physical features since it is the base of bodily activity. Again, one may map color, texture, and material, which can be reduced to some simple dichotomy like paved-unpaved. Since the floor is, above all, an activity surface, recording its slope and its discontinuities will indicate where one cannot easily stand or move. Where and when is it too rough, slippery, wet, broken, dusty, eroded, or steep? Where are the barriers to movement—for vehicles and for persons? A telling analysis can be made of floors dangerous to the blind or those inaccessible to a wheelchair (see Fig. 42). A complete evaluation of the facilities for the movement of pedestrians or cyclists should certainly be added to those so commonly made for motorists. What delays and detours are imposed on these second-class travelers? Floors can be characterized as to maintenance: their state of repair or cleanliness can be mapped by classes along some explicit scale. Analyses of this kind will lead directly to issues of repair, maintenance, access, and concern for the pedestrian or the disabled.

Information

The crucial role of communication in the city has been discussed. Environmental information, however, is rarely analyzed. Subjective references are common enough, but there are few examples of a systematic survey. Would it be possible, for example, to map the density of visible, explicit information? (In bits per acre?) This certainly can be done impressionistically, picking out the regions of overload, or of extreme underload, or simply the areas of stimulus and of calm. Visible information can be classified by the type of presentation or type of message (see Fig. 43) or can be characterized as to its legibility (140). The relative dominance of certain priority information—such as traffic signals—can be mapped. Signs may be divided between "rooted" and "unrooted," that is, whether they are related to their location or not. Passersby can be queried to see how well they read the scene and how this information affects them.

The public availability of selected information can be recorded. For example, where is a driver or a pedestrian clearly oriented as to his location and the location of nearby destinations? Where can he tell the time? Where can he learn about the ecology of a place or its social composition? At times it might be useful to map certain symbolic objects, such as flags and church towers, or to locate more subtle, implicit communications (keep out, come in, cheap, expensive, we and they, and so on), or to pinpoint the location and intensity of graffiti. It can be useful to locate the communications facilities available to the public: telephones, alarms, mailboxes, notice boards, public radios.

Natural Features

This is a familiar set of environmental features that are always
highly valued. (We ignore the curious implication that man-made
things are unnatural.) It is always fundamental to map the character of the land: its topography, water, and surface texture. Land
character is a basic element of regional quality. In large areas such
an analysis can be condensed to a division of the region into districts of similar land character ("broken, rocky, tangled growth";
"level, grassy, open"). To the classification by land character may
be added a classification by the dominant plant associations. These
characteristics are not to be confused with an ecological analysis,
which would trace the functional connections of the living system
with its physical setting and would quantify the energy flows.
Here, I am simply describing the perceptible results of that energy
exchange.

Natural factors that are particularly striking to the senses may be
emphasized. Landform can be analyzed by the visual compartments it produces or by its military crests. The texture and type of
tree cover and its relative sensitivity to visual intrusion can be
shown. Studies of predominant plantings may lead to statements
about the preferred landscape character of new development or to
plans for the location and type of street trees *(158)*. Places from
which wide expanses of sky can be seen, or where water, rock, and
earth are locally visible, or where one can hear the sounds that we
associate with "nature" may be noted. It is often important to
map those special places which should be conserved because of
their unique, fragile, or specially desirable, natural sensuous character. Studies of natural features are useful not only for conservation but also for setting district guidelines for development *(50)*.
These analyses can be applied to cities, just as well as to the countryside, a possibility often ignored because of the illusion that
cities and nature are separate phenomena *(161)*.

Visible Activity

Above all, people are interested in other people. Perceptible human activity is sometimes ignored in design studies, although it is such an obvious feature in the scenery that we attend to. The most general way to record this is to map the apparent density of generalized visible activity as it varies during the day. The mapping may be impressionistic or based on some measure such as visible persons per unit area of visible space. This is quite different from the activity density proper to a land use study. An office area of very high "objective" density may *seem* empty, particularly at certain hours, while the narrow streets of a mixed residential area, of much lower "real" density, will apparently be bursting with life.

The rhythm of visible activity should also be noted: What places are active throughout the entire night? Which are busy only in the early morning or only on holidays (see Fig. 44)? A diagrammatic movie, which recorded the pulsation of visible activity in a region, might be an ideal format for this information but could be too complex to follow. Visible activity can also be characterized as to type and as to the grain of the mix between distinct types of action or participant (places used by all the family, teenage hangouts, upper-income preserves). Visible flows of people, as well as localized activity, can be shown. Map diagrams can be supplemented by photographs or movies of the activity at selected places, as described later. Some degree of analysis of the visible activity, like some characterization of the spatial, temporal, and sequential form, is always essential in describing the sense of a region.

Certain special features of the sensed activity may be brought out. For example, where is the environment "transparent"; that is, where can the public see or hear the processes of production or of domestic life, or the activity taking place on private land and indoors? Perception may be direct (a building under construction) or indirect (a television screen showing the operation of an internal factory floor). In addition, a setting carries perceptual traces of human presence: trampled fields, laundry on a line, night lights burning, the toys of children, the smell of last night's cooking, or the personal modifications of a setting. Mapping the density of these traces might provide an index of the subjective "warmth" or "sense of life" of different areas.

Locations used for special celebrations, as well as parade routes, the place where the paseo occurs, or the places given special holiday decorations, can be noted. Perceptual indices of social territory can be mapped, and such visible features as fences, gates, hedges, pavement markings, signs, furniture, the types of stores, and the ways people cluster can be detailed. In reverse, one can map the "open" territories, those places so empty of others, so remote from control, that a person feels alone there and free to act at will. These are the back alleys, rooftops, waste grounds, wilderness, dumps, tidal flats, and so on.

Spatial Behavior

To understand the sensed environment, we must look at two human aspects of it: how people conceive it and how they act in it. The latter is the more objective, straightforward analysis, although it is not always easy to pick out the relevant acts from the flood of observable ones. In contrast to the preceding section, which considered visible activity simply as part of the scenery, this discussion focuses on the nature of behavior as a way of evaluating the quality of environment directly, in terms of the behavior itself. The commonsense procedure is to watch a place at length—perhaps to join in its activity—and then to summarize that activity verbally, noting its rhythmic changes and who does the acting (194). The description can be supplemented by photographs (75). The method needs patience and a good eye for relevance. It uses up time and good field observers.

Generalized observation can be sharpened by looking for particular kinds of action, which can then be represented diagrammatically. For example, one may concentrate on the movement of people and look for the things that influence that movement: the behavior at decision points, the barriers and the attractants, the origins and destinations, the involuntary delays and detours, the wayfinding behavior, the maintenance of personal space while moving, movement conflicts, and so on. One can look at territorial behavior or for the location and nature of meeting places. One may identify, map, time, and characterize the mosaic of behavior settings, that is, the localities in which repetitive social behavior is associated with specific kinds of spatial settings. This type of behavioral analysis is thus directly linked to the physical analysis of setting, described earlier, under the subheading "Typical Settings." A list of characteristic behavior settings conveys much of the sense of a place, especially to someone familiar with the culture. Given various criteria of adequacy, one can map an area by dividing it into settings in which there is an adequate or inadequate fit between behavior and form, or one may detect a shortage of some desired setting.

One may focus on a notation of each occasion when people make some tangible use of the physical setting, other than for walking or standing: Where do they sit, lie, lean against something, handle something? Still another possibility is to record "misfits" systematically: all the occasions when the setting can be seen to have given some direct, visible trouble to its users—as evidenced by accidents, delays, slips, squintings, grimaces, fumblings, and so on. Or one may look for the traces of human action left on the setting: trails, worn places, minor modifications. Selective observation makes for pointed analysis.

Instead of looking for selected behavior in one place over an extended period of time, the analyst may try to record what everyone is doing there at some particular moment. These momentary observations can be repeated in a regular way to give a sample of the total local activity. Again, the activity must be classified, to make the data manageable. A simple verbal schedule may be filled in: How many people here at this moment are talking, sleeping, eating, or fighting? (First, of course, one stops to think why one wants to know. Otherwise, one may find that the number of fighters is just a number.) Behavioral data in this instance are usually more relevant to the purpose if recorded as spatial phenomena, using a diagram that shows the type of action and its location, the type of actor, the relation to setting, and how this is changing, all in one complete expression (see Fig. 45). Such diagrams should be amplified by photographs and verbal pictures. A temporal series of them can be made for each place.

Brief bursts of motion pictures are quite informative about specific human actions and can be rerun at will for study (194). Long-focal-length cameras allow observation at a distance. Time-lapse movies are useful to compress the long-cycle rhythm of activity into a comprehensible pattern. The essence of how some place is used throughout the day can then be displayed in a single ten-minute film.

Instead of centering the observation on a single place, a record can be made of what individuals or groups do as they move from place to place. This is Perin's "behavior circuit," the unit of activity taken from the standpoint of the person (148). People may be accompanied on their daily round or tracked from a distance. Their actions can then be shown on a behavioral route map. Or they may be asked to keep a diary of what they did during a sample period or to recall what they did very recently. Before a photograph, sketch, or model of a locality, they discuss what they normally do there or predict what others like or unlike themselves might do there.

Analyses of environmental behavior are increasing but are not yet common. They are still usually confined to small, well-defined localities, where they have proved their usefulness. But there is no reason that these techniques should not be used in regional work. Group range maps could be prepared, and social territories delineated, if one were concerned with equality of access. On the other hand, the pattern of misfits in a typical place, or a diagram of selected behavior there, would be an excellent basis for policy as to its design.

Images

If one side of the coin is the actual behavior of people in a place, the other side is their internal image of it, how they picture it to themselves, what they feel about it, what it means to them. This is the darker side of the coin, but also the richer one, for our purpose. Some of these meanings and feelings may be analyzed indirectly. One can make a content analysis of newspapers, journals, and guidebooks or extract and synthesize the references to place in local literature (179). One may examine paintings, movies, or interpretative photographs. Artists and writers are sensitive registers of our deep feelings about places. A researcher will also find some gross indications in the history of political conflicts over environment or in the trend of economic values.

Our basic source of information, however, is direct dialogue with people, and this is a source that should never be neglected in any analysis of seemliness. Residents should be interviewed about their conceptions of a locality, what parts of it they use, what parts they can identify, and how they organize them (7, 55, 56, 62, 71, 82, 90, 91, 110, 111, 113, 126, 127, 128, 132, 133, 134, 136, 164, 166, 173, 175, 176). Verbal results may be tabulated, and the interview itself can be recorded audially or on videotape. Subjects can be asked to map a region or to sketch typical places, and these maps and sketches can be summarized quantitatively, qualitatively, and graphically, either to represent a general public image or to show the comparative image of some group (see Fig. 46).

People may be taught mapping technique, to enrich their expression in that medium *(90)*. Photograph recognition tests can be given. Similar interviews can be conducted on site or as the subject is walking or driving along. An interview in motion may record actions as well as what is said: the hesitations of a driver, the eye movements of a pedestrian. Passengers in a vehicle may be asked to make hurried sketches of what they see as they pass, in order to glean some of their fundamental impressions (see Fig. 47). People may be stopped in the street in order to be asked for the description of a place and how to get there. Aspects of the image of a region may even be distilled from written questionnaires and maps solicited by mail, on television, or through a newspaper campaign *(1, 94)*. In this way the net can be broadly cast, although the tastiest fish may escape.

These are ways of asking people to externalize their mental conception of the environment, and the results can be cross-checked, compared, and presented verbally and graphically. Which techniques to use depends on issues and resources. The structure of the actual landscape may then be compared to these mental structures, to see how the former is used, ignored, or distorted (see Fig. 48). Common ways of mentally structuring the region set a framework for physical strategies of improving environmental legibility. Common confusions reveal the trouble spots. The unknown, "empty" zones of the mental image may suggest underutilization or a failure of access, while the vividly known, "well-filled" places are resources to be conserved. New roads or other linear barriers should be diverted to the edges of commonly delineated home territories, to prevent disruption of these mental domains. These psychological neighborhoods (see Fig. 49) may also indicate the workable units for community organization and improvement *(166)*.

Environmental images are organized structures of recognition and relationship. They are also suffused with meaning, feeling, and value, and these meanings are more complex and subtle than are the dry bones of structure *(99, 124, 151)*. The investigator may map the areas where a person feels at home or alien, safe or unsafe, weak or powerful, warm or cold, pleased or disgusted. He may ask people to describe features or places in a free way or in terms of preselected polar adjectives—pleasant/unpleasant, active/ passive, strong/weak, interesting/boring, poor/rich, old/new, dirty/ clean, ordered/confused, dense/empty, and so on *(126)*. Better yet, the interviewer will encourage people to express their own dimensions for distinguishing value, as they describe their sense of the important differences between places, rather than forcing them to use dimensions imposed on them *(90)*. He may ask someone to outline his home area, to locate the territories of others, or to rank different places in terms of their symbolic importance (the latter ranking will make an interesting comparison with the actual visual dominance of places). Residents can be asked to name the ugliest places in town or the most beautiful ones, to rank places in order of preference, or to say how they would like to see them changed. They can be queried about their understanding of the past history of a place, or about the future changes they expect to occur there, and whether that past or that imagined future has any relevance to themselves.

Discussions can be prompted by photographs or sketches *(80)*. These pictures can be chosen or doctored in various ways to uncover the landscape features that are strongly associated with feelings *(159)*. Interviews are often fruitful if conducted on the site. Even better, the person may be asked to give the researcher a guided tour—a tour that can be recorded, put on videotape, or illustrated with photographs taken on the spot, to be discussed again later. Early memories of the landscape or dreams for the future may be evoked (see Fig. 51). People may be asked to construct utopias or cacotopias, to play imaginary roles, to act out situations on models of the environment, to weave stories around untitled pictures, or to guess the kinds of people associated with various pictured landscapes. These techniques produce rich material, some of it straightforward, some of it less reliable (particularly when one is dealing with wishes and predictions). But if the different insights are correlated for consistency, the results are illuminating. The data are typically qualitative rather than quantitative, often best shown in diagrams, or in "speaking landscapes" (sketches with verbal comments appended directly to the locations where they were made, or about which they were made), or as a selection of the orignial materials: photographs, drawings, videotape, interview tape (see Figs. 5 and 50).

Summary Evaluations

The complexity of these data must be reduced to some manageable form. To organize data by place seems intuitively sensible, and it is an easy way to communicate findings to the general public. A particular square will be studied in terms of a whole range of criteria, or the network of public spaces will be investigated as a whole but only in terms of a few selected items. The regional sensory study of the island of Martha's Vineyard, for example, was organized into two parts: the character of the typical visual districts into which the island might be divided and the character of the main road system—its views, its typical segments, and its connectivity as a whole. (Although classifying a region into a set of distinct districts is a familiar kind of analysis, classifying road segments by their sensory qualities, as in Fig. 23, may seem strange.) For both districts and roads, the emphasis was on their qualities of identity (that is, recognizable character or memorability), since the principal motive of the study was the conservation of existing character. Such a division of a landscape into "places" and "journeys" is a very natural one (50).

A city can be analyzed in detail, neighborhood by neighborhood, with citywide considerations superimposed. Or a single large feature may be studied, as in the British report on the visual environs of the Thames (see Fig. 53) or the analysis of the Rio Grande passing through Albuquerque, New Mexico *(17, 52)*. One can look into some chosen repetitive element: the landscape of signs, for example, or the mass transit system, with its cars, routes, and stations, or the citywide use of trees and vegetation, or the city "floor."

Attempts are being made to compute composite environmental indices for the districts of a region, so that areas can be ranked overall and resources for improvement can be allotted rationally, or with the appearance of rationality *(19, 199)*. All qualities must then be expressed as a single unit of cost and benefit, such as dollars (how many dollars for a safe crossing and the smell of roses?), or they must be ranked along abstract scales and then weighted for their relative importance, which comes to the same thing (see Fig. 52). Physical quantities can be converted to normalized scales; for other factors a scale of five is popular, since it corresponds to the obvious verbal classification of indifferent in the middle, very good and bad at the extremes, and rather in between. Weightings between factors can be devised by asking people to rank those factors by pairs or by aggregating the opinions of "experts," and they may then be multiplied by the number of people affected (and this number can also be weighted by *its* relative importance). Weightings, scales, and classifications are all arbitrary. As they shift, the index jumps.

A simpler technique for constructing a composite index is to score areas for the number of times they fall below explicit thresholds of tolerance for the various qualities being analyzed. But environmental qualities are rarely so black and white as those sharp thresholds imply. Moreover, a weighting must still be used. Thus, while of some use in the early stages of an evaluation, composite indices are not very trustworthy. At present, it seems that we do better to present achievements and costs for each factor in the form or language suited to that factor, along with an account of who is affected and how those affected people judge the relative importance of that factor. The composite evaluative decision remains intuitive, but at least it is based on data clearly set forth. None of the preceding is intended as an attack on measurement, where feasible, or on standards or areawide comparisons. It is the attempt to construct one all-embracing measure of quality, precise and suitable for all occasions, that seems so dubious. But it is simple and useful to map areas that are below some standard of protection from summer heat and glare, for example, or to compare two places for the frequency of their views of the sea. Comparative environmental indicators of that kind make inequalities of seemliness explicit in a very useful way.

Another way of generalizing the data is by persons rather than by places. That is, a series of drawings and descriptions will convey the image of the regional landscape which is held by significant groups of its inhabitants, as well as the actual use they make of it and the problems and pleasures they find in it (see Fig. 46). The correspondences and contrasts between these group patterns can be highlighted. Ways in which the conceptions and range of key groups are changing may be emphasized.

Yet another approach is to collect information related to the satisfaction of some basic criterion. That is, one pulls together an analysis of communication in the city, or of the visible presence of nature, or of the range of climatic comfort in the region.

Finally, a study may summarize its findings about a region as a set of actions to be taken. For example, features to be conserved are distinguished from those to be changed and those to be replaced (see Fig. 54). Sensory conditions that would be difficult or costly to modify are contrasted with those on which public action could have substantial effect. Substandard areas and sensory problems, as well as the potentialities for improvement, are selected (see Fig. 55). Or the study may be organized in terms of an oper-

ating agency or of the means of implementation: the visual consequence of a zoning ordinance, the sensory form of city parks or
state highways, the seemliness of subsidized housing. This is an excellent organization for the purpose of stimulating immediate action. Choice of data structure, like the selection of criteria or processes, depends on motives, constraints, and clients.

Flexible systems for storing and managing these representations
of sensory quality are still lacking. One should be able to call up
the sense pattern of an area along with its population characteristics, or to match the traffic flow of a highway network to its visual
sequences, or to see how changing ownership relates to shifts in
visible maintenance. Sense data are traditionally gathered as if
they were in a sealed compartment, incompatible with other concerns. They are surveyed spasmodically and stored permanently.
Ideally, they should be recorded in replaceable chunks, which
could be integrated into maps and other comprehensive descriptions on demand but which could also be replaced or manipulated
for different purposes. The data would be "objective," not in the
sense that subjective perception and feeling would be excluded
(for they are at the heart of our matter), but in the sense that
informed observers would reliably report the same data from the
same situation. This requirement implies the systematic training of
observers, explicit procedures, frequent spot checks, and regular
discussions of comparative findings.

Computer storage is possible for place-specific data, such as
sound levels at different locations. One can also imagine collec-
tions of slides, coded by location, which could be called up or replaced as needed, or short runs of film or videotape that characterize sequences or activities. But sensory data are frequently dynamic (the changes of light), sufficiently elusive (a local smell), subjective (the meaning of a place), or so due to action at a distance (a
panorama) or by their nature integrated (a long sequence) that
they resist division into discrete small pieces codable by location,

by social group, or by any other single dimension. Records of sensory data, at least for some time, may be expected to remain in hybrid form and to be less than systematic. But some subtlety in the information can be sacrificed to make it as receptive to new input as possible. Like any first-round description, the general sensory analysis of a region will be far from exhaustive. Preliminary surveys are mostly a way of finding out what is knowable and relevant. In their eagerness to be comprehensive, planning agencies gather many irrelevant data. The question to ask is: "If I knew that, would it really change what I do?" Moreover, we inevitably change our minds about what we want to know.

In any event, an agency should establish some continuing record of the sensory state of its area, in a form that can be connected to action. Maps and diagrams will indicate localities where there are substandard conditions. Programs will target specific improvements to be made within particular periods, including the required budget and responsibility. Diagnoses of the sensory state and definite programs for its improvement should be open to the public. Sensory analyses would be part of the information to be used when modifications to a place are designed or when designs are reviewed. They would also be a primary input for writing a design program, that is, for specifying what sense qualities will be required in any acceptable solution.

Findings and recommendations in studies of environmental quality are often communicated in elaborately designed publications, written in formal language and filled with complex maps and highly finished illustrations. The design talent which was unable to find an effective vent in the complicated, slow-changing region has turned its force into creating a book. These brochures are impressive, and they often have an air of finality about them. They are expensive; they daunt the reader. Furthermore, they distance him from an experience or a concern that is common to everyone and about which he will have important things to say. In contrast, a more informal presentation will encourage a dialogue. It can consist of rough sketches drawn on the spot at local meetings or of slides that include views taken by local people as well as professionals, or it may be communicated in newspaper or television accounts that solicit comments, or in public on-site tours, or by the posting of an analysis at the location itself.

When the preceding collection of techniques is reviewed, it becomes clear that some of them can be used in almost every situation (the general analyses of site, settlement form, behavior, and image, for example), while others are employed only when particular issues arise. Some surveys are simple and easy to conduct (a survey of the cleanliness of the public floor), while others are difficult to define, however important they may be (analyzing whether environmental communications are conducive to personal development). Some studies are directly connected to policy and action (barriers to the handicapped), while others are linked to policy in only a tenuous way (the texture of artificial light in the city, which we may feel is important but do not know how to manage or even if we should try to do so). Some are only descriptions of an exogenous state (the general climate), while others refer to characteristics that can be manipulated, predicted, and designed (the form of a public space).

This group of methods is simply a collection; there is no organized theory for dealing with sensory data. The techniques vary widely in their immediate usefulness and their state of development. On the other hand, it would surely have been an error to pass over all those methods whose details or whose applications have yet to be clarified.

One major difficulty is that there is no integrated language that is suitable for use in regional sensory studies. The architectural language (of section, plan, and elevation) is powerful because, once understood, it can be used to record a building, to design it, to predict its (architectural) performance, and to guide its construction. It can be used sketchily or with great precision. So strong and inclusive is this language that it tends to take over even when sensory form is analyzed at a regional scale. Unfortunately, it is inappropriate because of the size and complexity of regional phenomena, their constant cyclical and secular change, the importance of human activity and human images, the continuity of regional management, and the multiplicity of factors involved. Yet the standard verbal, numerical, legal, and mapping languages of regional discourse are even less adequate to our purpose. A unified language appropriate to the sensory form of regions will be a long time developing, if indeed a unified language is possible. Meanwhile, we must deal with the many different aspects of this issue in diverse, and sometimes not entirely compatible, ways. Language in some form—whether graphic, verbal, gestural, mathematical, or whatever— is indispensible to thought.

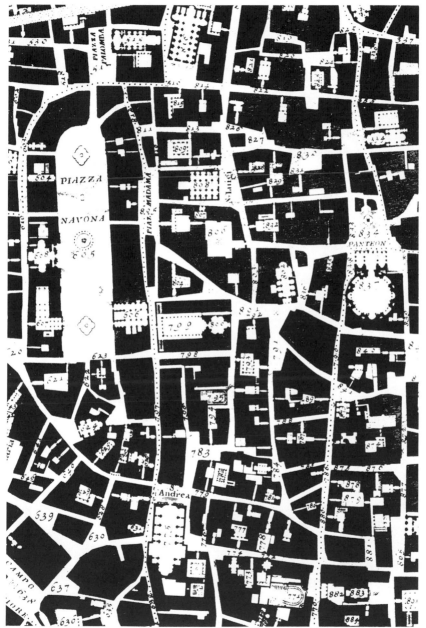

15 Nolli's building coverage map of Rome in 1748 conveys the intricate texture of streets, piazzas, church interiors, palaces, courts, and gardens.

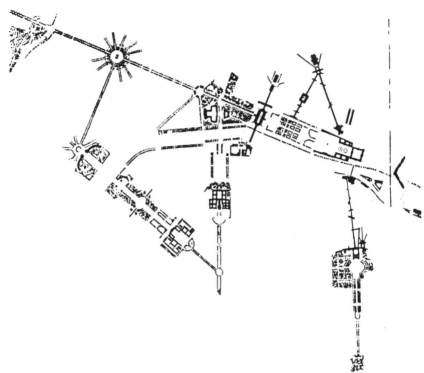

16 A diagram of the essential spatial structure of central Paris: the great open spaces and major visual axes.

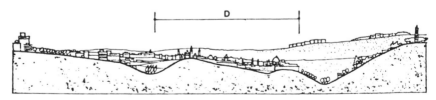

17 A section through the Old City of Jerusalem *(D)* shows its relation to the surrounding hills.

18 An isometric view of central Jerusalem.

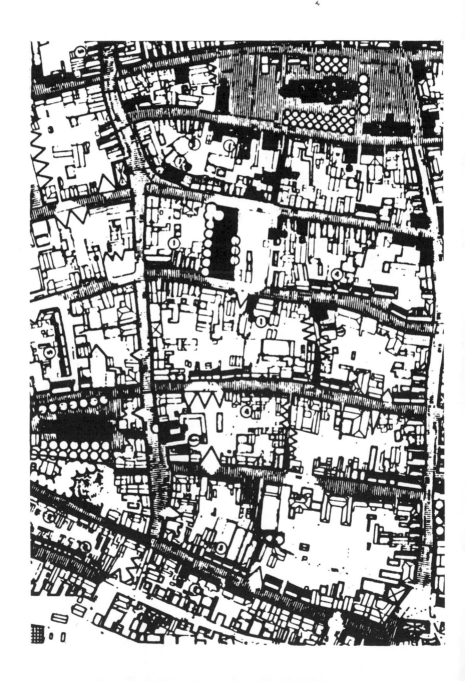

⌐‾‾‾‾⌐	solid row of buildings
🏚️🏠	row of single buildings: facades and roof forms to be maintained
▰▰▰	historic structures
▰▰ D	under legal protection
⊔⊓⊔	intermittent spacial definition
⊔ ⊔ ⊔	street space defined by freestanding buildings
∧∧∧	spatial definition missing
⊔⊔⊔⊔⊔	sloping riverbank
⊓⊓⊓⊓⊓	dam
⌐‾‾‾⌐	bridge
▥▥▥	square, street space
▓▓▓	narrow lane
⬜	open park
▦▦▦	inaccessible area
▭	freestanding structure
⊠	building out of scale
◆	tower visible at a distance
●	chimney
①	half-timbered building, 17th-19th century
②	slate burgher's house, classic period
③	slate row house, classic period
④	plaster double house, late classic
▦	open field
○	single tree, natural landmark
∞	solid mass of trees
○○○	avenue of trees
ᴧᴧᴧᴧ	shrubbery, wooded edge

19 A detailed spatial analysis of the central area of the town of Lippstadt, in Germany.

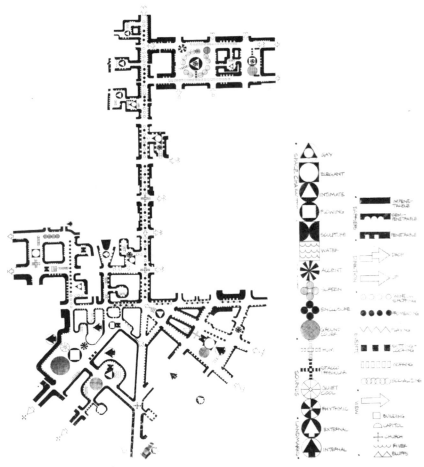

20 A spatial analysis of a portion of Minneapolis that records subjective impressions as well as physical objects.

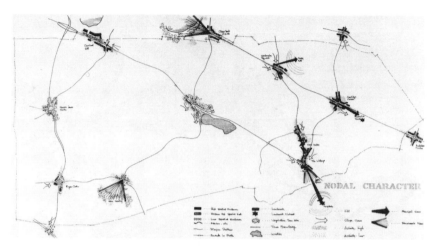

21   The structure of Brookline, Massachusetts, is analyzed by a description
of its principal focal points.

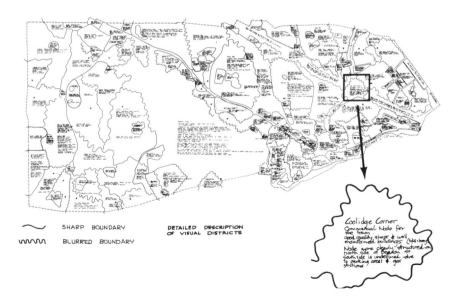

SHARP BOUNDARY   DETAILED DESCRIPTION
                         OF VISUAL DISTRICTS
BLURRED BOUNDARY

Coolidge Corner Commercial Node for the town good quality, shops & well maintained buildings (1-4 story) Node more clearly structured on north side of Beacon St. south side is undefined - due to parking areas & gas stations

22   The town of Brookline is further classified into visually similar districts.

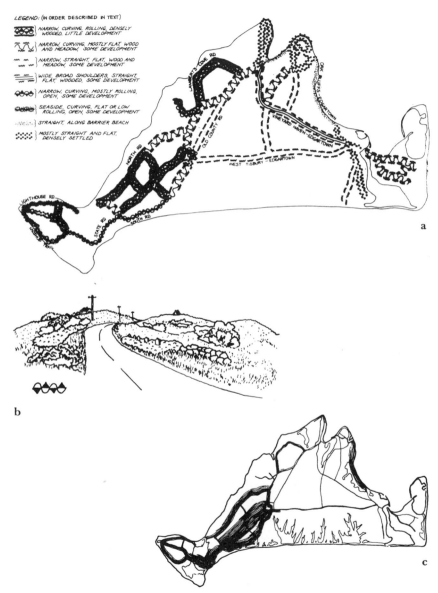

LEGEND: (IN ORDER DESCRIBED IN TEXT)

NARROW, CURVING, ROLLING, DENSELY WOODED, LITTLE DEVELOPMENT

NARROW, CURVING, MOSTLY FLAT, WOOD AND MEADOW, SOME DEVELOPMENT

NARROW, STRAIGHT, FLAT, WOOD AND MEADOW, SOME DEVELOPMENT

WIDE, BROAD SHOULDERS, STRAIGHT, FLAT, WOODED, SOME DEVELOPMENT

NARROW, CURVING, MOSTLY ROLLING, OPEN, SOME DEVELOPMENT

SEASIDE, CURVING, FLAT OR LOW ROLLING, OPEN, SOME DEVELOPMENT

STRAIGHT, ALONG BARRIER BEACH

MOSTLY STRAIGHT AND FLAT, DENSELY SETTLED

a

b

c

23a,b,c   Road landscapes on Martha's Vineyard, classified by type, and an example of one type. For comparison, a mapping of preferred roads; note the correspondence of preferences to road type.

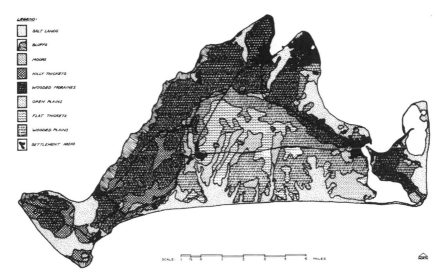

24 The island of Martha's Vineyard, mapped into the eight landscape types
whose policy implications were tabulated in Figure 10.

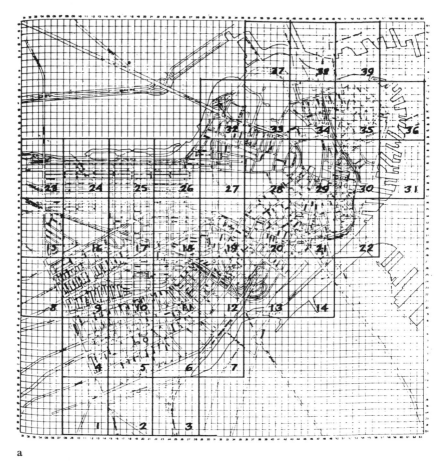

a

25a,b The layout of a photogrid on central Boston and some of the photographs of square 28, covering parts of Beacon Hill, the Common, and the downtown retail area.

b

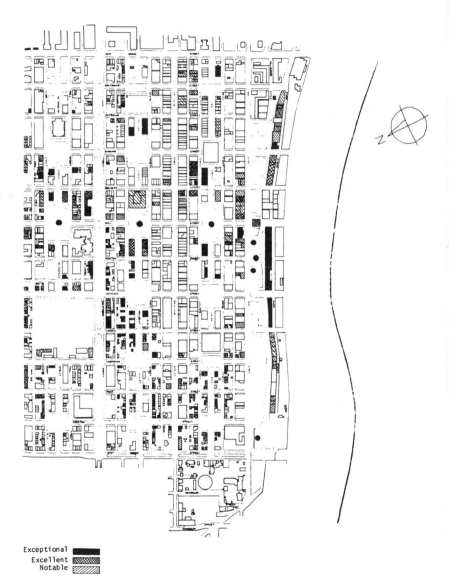

Exceptional
Excellent
Notable

26   Significant historic architecture in Savannah.

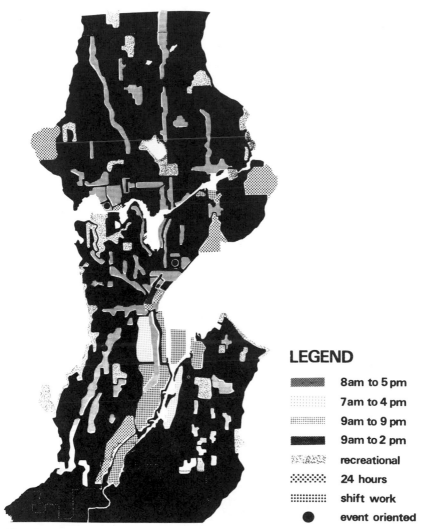

LEGEND

▬▬▬ 8am to 5 pm

▓▓▓ 7am to 4 pm

▦▦▦ 9am to 9 pm

▬▬▬ 9am to 2 pm

▒▒▒ recreational

▨▨▨ 24 hours

▥▥▥ shift work

● event oriented

27 The "time envelopes" of Seattle. The perception of parts of the city varies according to the time of day.

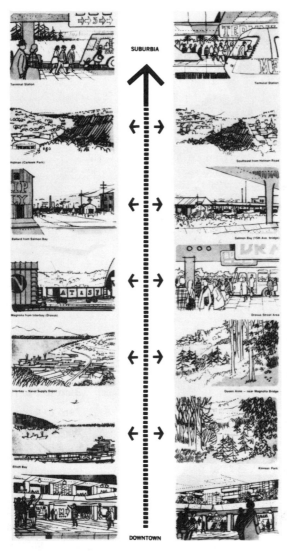

28 An analysis of a proposed transit line by
means of sketches of the principal views to be seen
to the left and right along the new route.

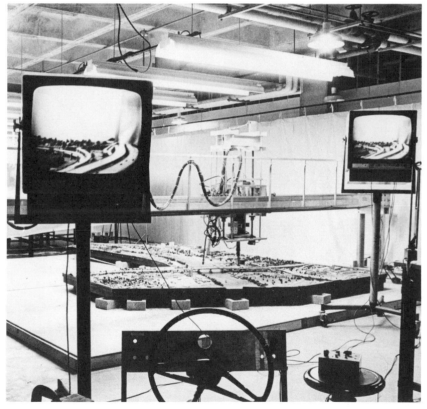

29 An environmental simulator allows one to "walk" or "drive" through a model, watching the view as it would appear on such a trip projected on a television screen.

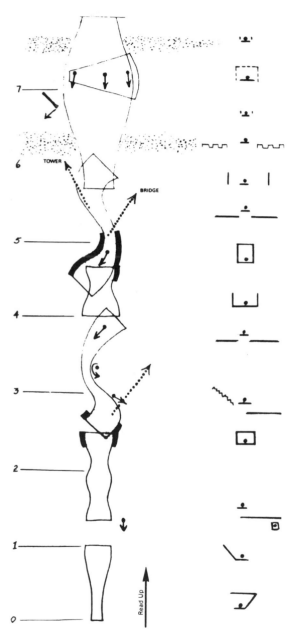

30 A diagram of the sense of space and motion along the Northeast Expressway in Boston.

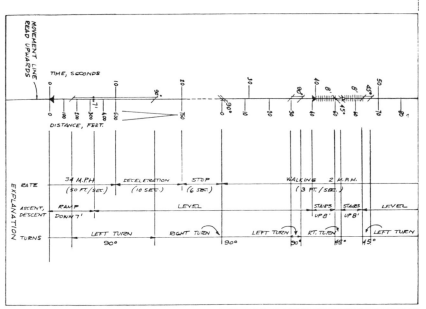

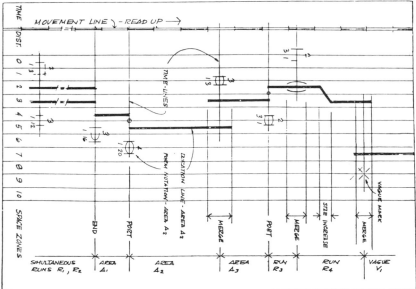

31 Thiel's more precise notation for the movement, duration, and space-form experienced along a sequence.

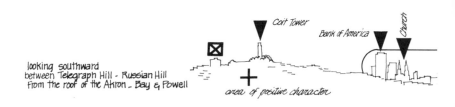

32 One of a series of composite photographs recording the panoramic views of San Francisco, with a diagram denoting and evaluating the principal elements to be seen.

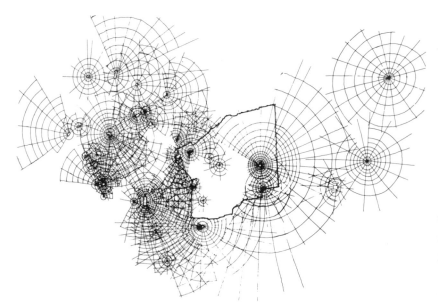

33 An abstract, composite diagram of visibility: the areas from which one can see the dominant skyline elements of Jerusalem.

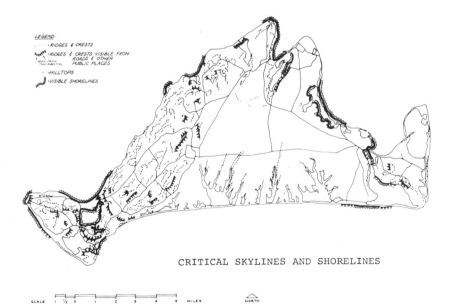

CRITICAL SKYLINES AND SHORELINES

34 Locating the ridges and shorelines that are frequently visible from public places on the island of Martha's Vineyard.

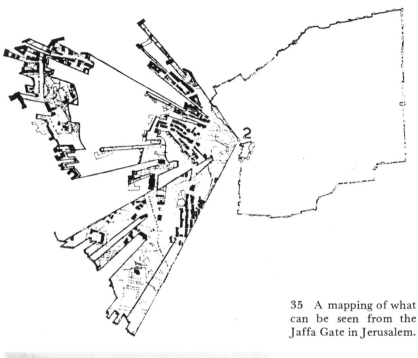

35 A mapping of what can be seen from the Jaffa Gate in Jerusalem.

36 Dividing a city into the areas seen and unseen is another way of describing its visibility. The regions of central Jerusalem marked A are the prominent skyline ridges; B, the areas not visible from major viewpoints; and C, the most visible open spaces.

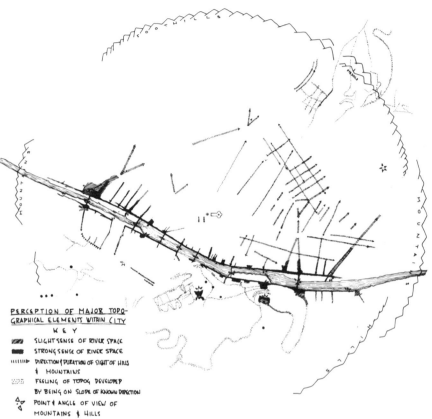

PERCEPTION OF MAJOR TOPO-
GRAPHICAL ELEMENTS WITHIN CITY
            K E Y
▰▰ SLIGHT SENSE OF RIVER SPACE
▬▬ STRONG SENSE OF RIVER SPACE
ıııııⱳ DIRECTION & DURATION OF SIGHT OF HILLS
       & MOUNTAINS
▒▒▒ FEELING OF TOPOG DEVELOPED
       BY BEING ON SLOPE OF KNOWN DIRECTION
△◁ POINT & ANGLE OF VIEW OF
◁   MOUNTAINS & HILLS

37 The locations in Florence, Italy, from which one can glimpse the surrounding hills, sense the space of the Arno River, or be aware of the slope of the ground. Thus certain sections of the city have a richer connection to the natural setting than do others.

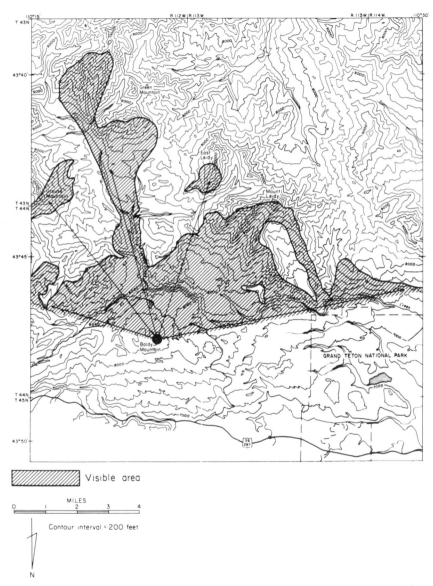

Visible area

MILES
0   1   2   3   4

Contour interval = 200 feet

N

38 An accurate mapping of a "viewshed," the terrain visible from a major
viewpoint in the Teton National Forest, Wyoming. Using this, foresters can
judge the visual effect of any proposed cutting of timber.

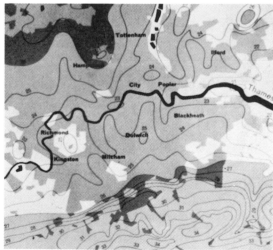

39 How elements of the climate of London vary over its region. In the map at top, contours show the percentage frequency of fog on winter mornings; below, contours show the inches of rain per year.

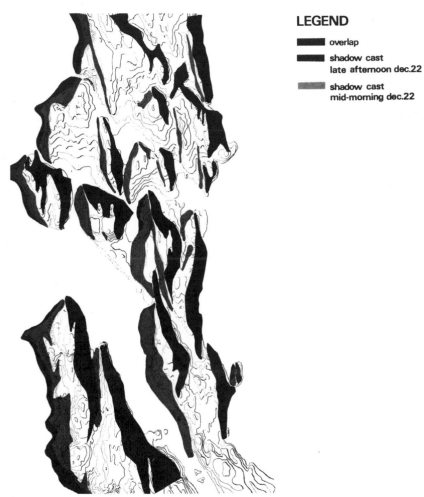

LEGEND

██████ overlap

██████ shadow cast
        late afternoon dec.22

▓▓▓▓▓▓ shadow cast
        mid-morning dec.22

40   Morning and afternoon shade in Seattle during the winter.

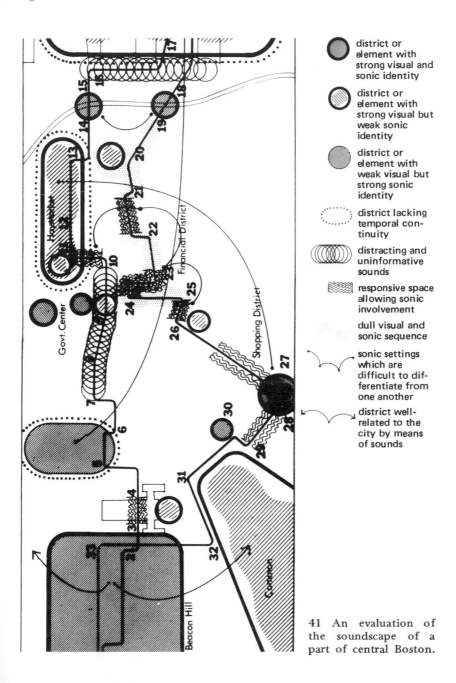

district or element with strong visual and sonic identity

district or element with strong visual but weak sonic identity

district or element with weak visual but strong sonic identity

district lacking temporal continuity

distracting and uninformative sounds

responsive space allowing sonic involvement

dull visual and sonic sequence

sonic settings which are difficult to differentiate from one another

district well-related to the city by means of sounds

41 An evaluation of the soundscape of a part of central Boston.

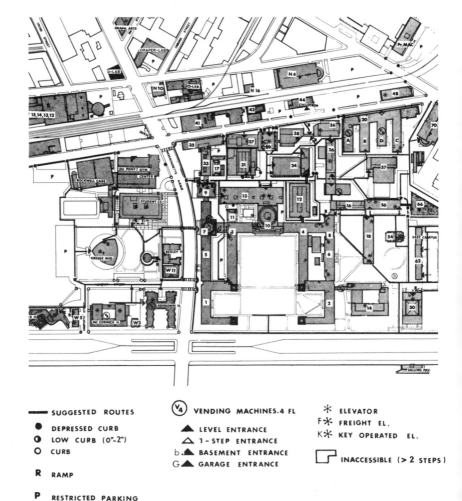

SUGGESTED ROUTES

● DEPRESSED CURB
◐ LOW CURB (0"-2")
○ CURB

R RAMP

P RESTRICTED PARKING

Ⓥ₄ VENDING MACHINES. 4 FL

▲ LEVEL ENTRANCE
△ 1-STEP ENTRANCE
b▲ BASEMENT ENTRANCE
G▲ GARAGE ENTRANCE

✳ ELEVATOR
F✳ FREIGHT EL.
K✳ KEY OPERATED EL.

⌐ INACCESSIBLE (> 2 STEPS)

42   A map of the barriers to the movement of wheelchairs through the central campus of the Massachusetts Institute of Technology.

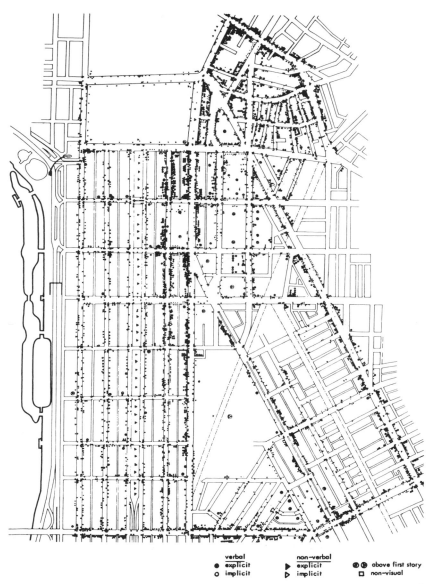

verbal		non-verbal			
●	explicit	▶	explicit	❶ ❶	above first story
○	implicit	▷	implicit	☐	non-visual

43 A systematic survey of the intentional signs in the Back Bay area of Boston. Note their number, their varying intensity, their repetitiveness, and how they cluster in the business districts and along the major motorways.

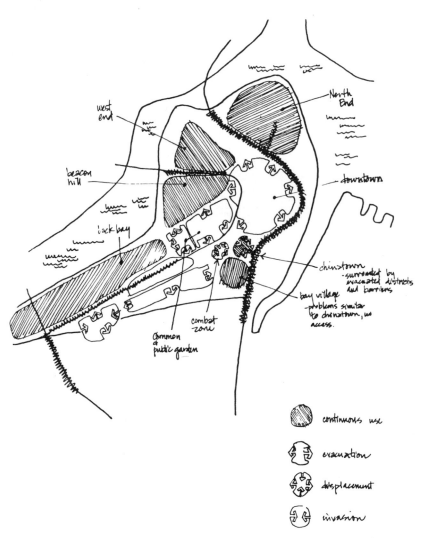

West
end

North
End

beacon
hill

downtown

back bay

chinatown
-surrounded by
evacuated districts
and barriers

bay village
-problems similar
to chinatown, no
access.

common
&
public garden

combat
zone

continuous use

evacuation

displacement

invasion

44   Cycles of use in central Boston: continuous, or empty at night ("evacuation"), or active especially at night ("invasion"), or shifting from day to night activity ("displacement").

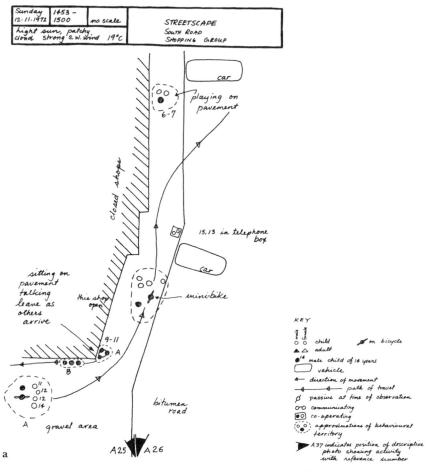

| Sunday 12·11·1972 | 1453 – 1500 | no scale | STREETSCAPE |
| light sun, patchy. cloud strong S.W. Wind 19°C | | | South Road SHOPPING GROUP |

car

playing on pavement

6-7

Closed shops

15,13 in telephone box

car

sitting on pavement talking leave as others arrive

this shop open

mini-bike

9-11

A

B

○¹¹
○ 12
● 12
○ 14

A gravel area

bitumen road

A 25   A 26

a

KEY

♂ male ♀ female ○ child   🚲 on bicycle
▲ △ adult
●¹⁴ male child of 14 years
⬭ vehicle
← direction of movement
◄─── path of travel
∅ passive at time of observation
○○ communicating
[●○] co-operating
(○ ○) approximations of behavioural territory
▶ A 37 indicates position of descriptive photo showing activity with reference number

45a,b Diagramming the shifting activity of a street in Melbourne, Australia. The photograph records one instant in this flow.

b

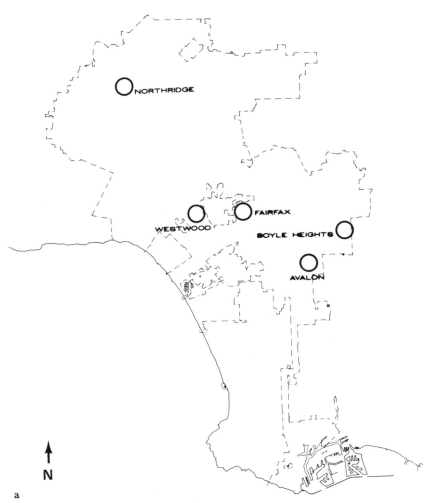

a

46a-f A comparison of the frequency with which the residents of five different areas in Los Angeles drew various elements of the urban region, when asked to make a map of it. The range and frequency of these elements (all reduced here to the same scale) are presumably an indication of the comparative knowledge and use of the region.

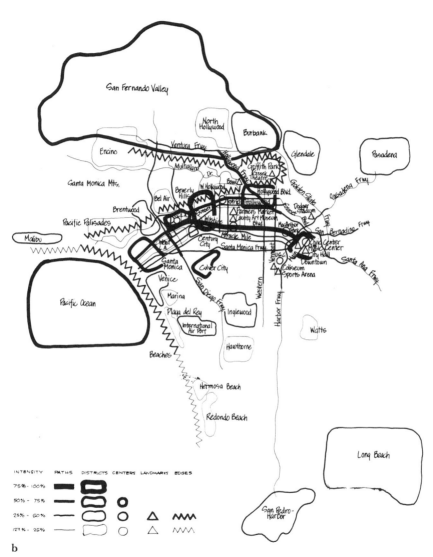

b

Westwood

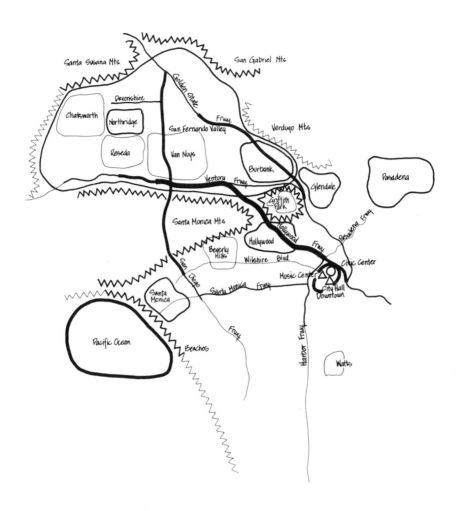

c

Northridge

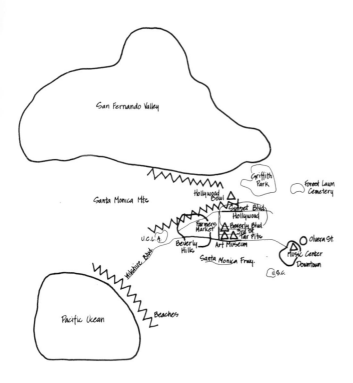

San Fernando Valley

Griffith Park

Santa Monica Mts.

Forest Lawn Cemetery

Hollywood Bowl

Sunset Blvd.
Hollywood

Farmers Market

Beverly Blvd.

3rd St.

Tar Pits

U.C.L.A.

Beverly Hills

Art Museum

Olvera St.

Music Center
Downtown

Wilshire Blvd.

Santa Monica Frwy.

U.S.C.

Pacific Ocean

Beaches

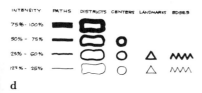

INTENSITY	PATHS	DISTRICTS	CENTERS	LANDMARKS	EDGES
75% - 100%					
50% - 75%					
25% - 50%					
12% - 25%					

d

Fairfax

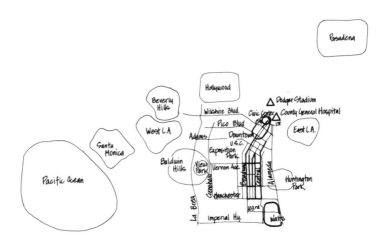

e

Avalon

City Hall   Union Station
Little Tokyo
Downtown   Brooklyn Ave.
Bus Depot

INTENSITY   PATHS   DISTRICTS   CENTERS   LANDMARKS   EDGES
75% - 100%
50% - 75%
25% - 50%
12% - 25%

f
Boyle Heights

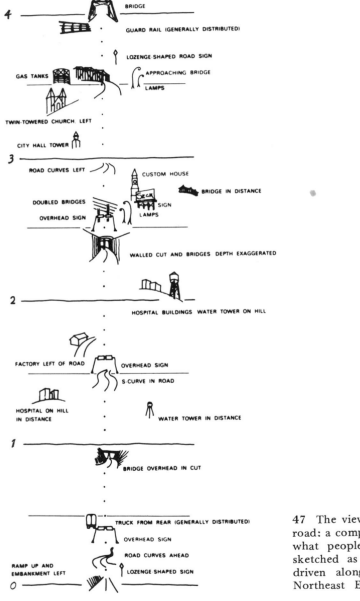

47 The view from the road: a compendium of what people hurriedly sketched as they were driven along Boston's Northeast Expressway.

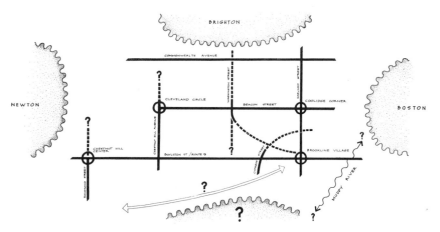

48 How the residents of Brookline, Massachusetts, tend to distort or to ignore parts of their community and its relation to the rest of the city.

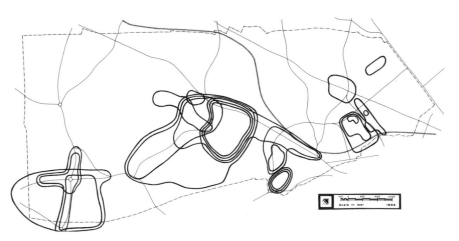

49 Residents of Brookline were asked to sketch their own neighborhoods.
When the boundaries of the areas they chose to draw are plotted on an accurate map, they reveal something about the social structure of the town, as
well as about its visual form.

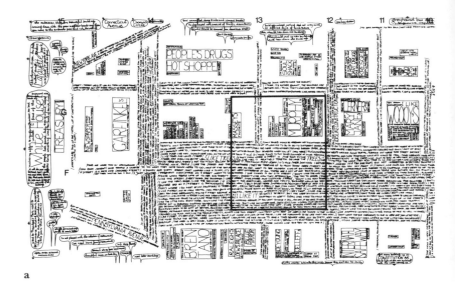

a

50a,b,c Washingtonians talk about their downtown business area.

MASSEYS FAVORITE

NOTHING IN MIND WHEN GOING DOWN / THERE WAS AN EMPTY STORE WHICH / LIKE THE SCENERY, LIKE THE STD

GARBACINI / ICE CREAM SHOP

KLEIN'S

DON'T LIKE HAHN'S VERY CONSERVATIVE

MURPHY'S

BEAUTIFUL / ALWAYS COME TO COULDN'T FIND WHAT I WANTED / DALMO DRESS STORE / GLEN MUSIC / BONDS STORE

STRECO

TODAY IT WAS TO RESTAURANT REEVES

RITZ

BAKERY

PHILLIPSBORN

SS/BUS INCONSISTENT/ IT /ONLY BUSSES SHOULD BE HERE/SORRY THEY DISCONTINUED MIN
T/WALKED THRU MALL /A LOT OF WALKING TO DO TO GO TO DIFFERENT STORES, P
ED, SEEMED SHADY/MALL HAS MADE IMPROVEMENTS /BECOMES BARGAIN ENTER, RUN
POST OFFICES GOOD, BUT SENSELESS WHEN YOU LET CARS HERE /PLAZA CONSTRU
AND DOWN F and G/MORE PLACES TO PUT BIKES /NUMBER OF SHOTS PLEASING
S/I DON'T KNOW WHERE G STREET IS /THE POOR DYING TREES; IT
/OK THE MALL IS RELATIVELY PEACEFUL BECAUSE THE TREES HE
ABOUT IT /TOO MUCH RIFF-RAFF /IT'S NICE /MESS /NOTHING I NOTICE
ATMOSPHERE /THEY'RE TEARING UP SO MUCH DOWN HERE, THERE'S N
NGS ARE ALL OLD; WANT TO SEE MODERN KIND OF BUILDINGS FOR CU
NOT VERY IMPRESSIVE AT ALL, THERE ARE A LOT OF OLD BUILDINGS, N
18 STORES / SHE THINKS 15 ON 11TH STREET / DON'T LIKE THE WAY TH
NOW; DOESN'T LIKE HOW THEY APPROACH YOU, THEY TRY TO GRAB /DO
F STREET, SHOE STORES AND CLOTHING STORES; DON'T LIKE HOW STRE
ASN'T FOR GARFINKEL, WOODIES AND MACY'S, BUSINESS WOULD BE 3RD
GET NOW /I BUY SHOES HERE /IMPROVING/TOO MANY PEOPLE AND ITS
JED, ARCHITECTURE IS REALLY BAD /TOO MANY PEOPLE /ALWAYS LOOK
ACTIVE/IN PHONE BOOTH NO PLACE TO SIT DOWN; NO PLACES TO SIT FARTHER I
TRAFFIC; MORE EVENING INTERESTS! /DIRTY, VERY DRAB, SHOPS ARE H
K; /SLIGHTLY DECREPIT, BUT HAS CHEAP DISCOUNT STO.
ED/I LIKE IT. NO EFFORT TO KEEP IT CLEAN; CARS MAKE TOO MUCH R
US HANGING AROUND; IF YOU WANT TO MAKE A CALL, YOU CAN; IF YOU WANT TO MAIL
OKING; DON'T LIKE UNCOMBED HAIR, DIRTY LEVIS /WILL WINDOW SHOP /BUILD IN
IN USED TO BE; SO MANY SHOPS HAVE LEFT, NICER SMALLER STORES ARE MOVIN
RENOVATION; SOME OF THESE OLD BUILDINGS SHOULD BE TORN DOWN, FOR EXAMT

b

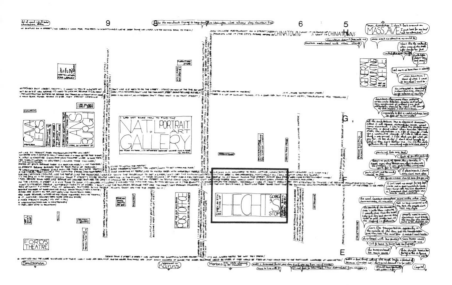

-DINGS OLD, NOWHERE TO PARK, OFFICES; LOOKS BAD/A
IN/THE AREA IS DELAPEDATED, THAT'S ABOUT ALL/SAW A
OPLE TO SIT DOWN ALONG THE STREET AND AT BUS STOP
IING THERE YOU WOULD WANT TO BUY/OPEN STORES OI
ENJOY THE STORES, GENERALLY I LIKE IT, I DON'T REALLY
THE OLD BUILDINGS, I DON'T LIKE THESE BOXES THAT THE

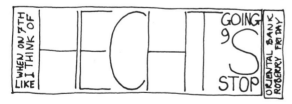

c

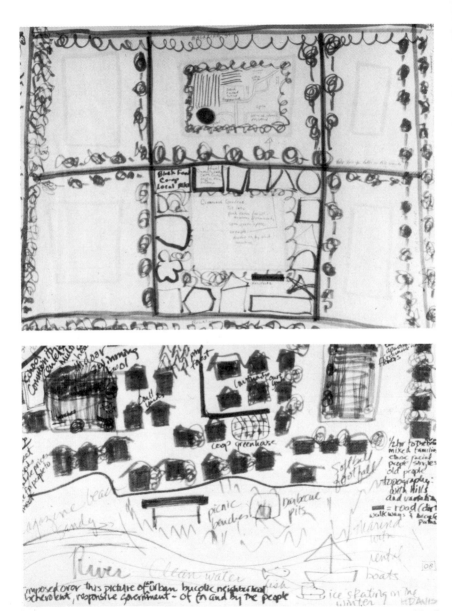

51 Local people in Cambridgeport, near Boston, dream about their ideal community.

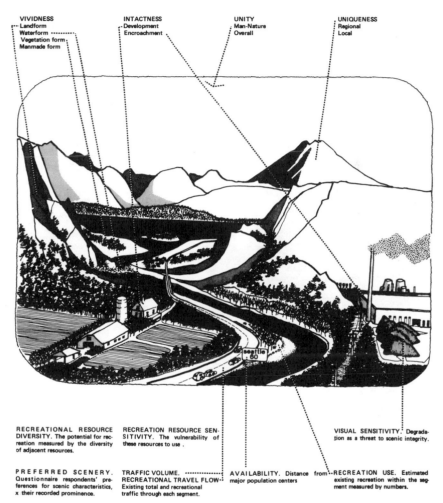

VIVIDNESS
Landform
Waterform
Vegetation form
Manmade form

INTACTNESS
Development
Encroachment

UNITY
Man-Nature
Overall

UNIQUENESS
Regional
Local

RECREATIONAL RESOURCE DIVERSITY. The potential for recreation measured by the diversity of adjacent resources.

RECREATION RESOURCE SENSITIVITY. The vulnerability of these resources to use .

VISUAL SENSITIVITY. Degradation as a threat to scenic integrity.

PREFERRED SCENERY. Questionnaire respondents' preferences for scenic characteristics, x their recorded prominence.

TRAFFIC VOLUME. RECREATIONAL TRAVEL FLOW Existing total and recreational traffic through each segment.

AVAILABILITY. Distance from major population centers

RECREATION USE. Estimated existing recreation within the segment measured by numbers.

52 A composite landscape sketch illustrating the criteria used in judging the relative scenic quality of Washington highways. Defined and applied by professionals, they are then combined into elaborate quantified indices.

outstanding area	
outstanding element	
positive element	
negative element	
negative area	

53 Part of a massive assessment of the visual environment of the Thames River, as it passes through the London region.

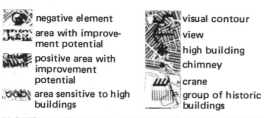

negative element

area with improvement potential

positive area with improvement potential

area sensitive to high buildings

visual contour

view

high building

chimney

crane

group of historic buildings

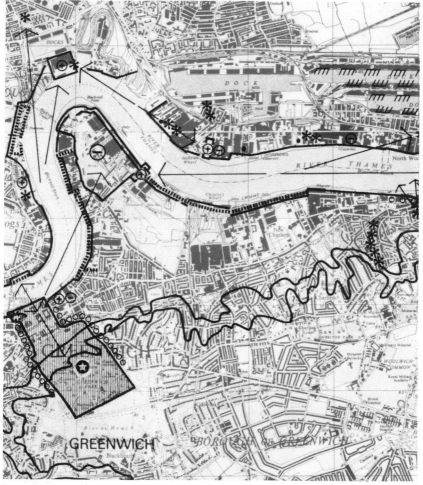

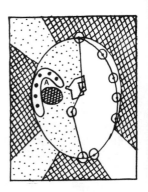

54 A simple diagram summarizing the visual structure of Jerusalem. The Old City is enclosed by ridges, but there are "windows" opening diagonally to the northwest, the southwest, and the southeast. The quality of the setting is particularly sensitive to any development on ridge *A*.

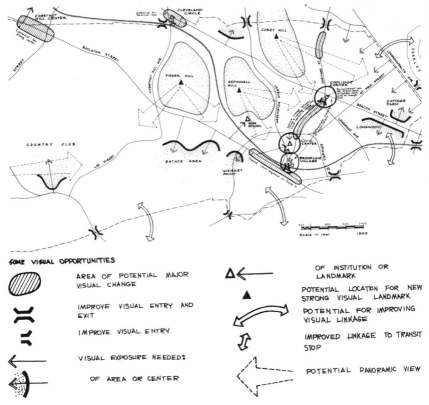

55 The visual opportunities in the town of Brookline: the field of action for public policy.

Appendix 3: Sources of Evidence

Any systematic study of the sense of the environment is rather recent. Only within the past few years have environmental psychologists, schools of architectural psychology, journals about environment and behavior, and associations of researchers in environmental design appeared *(54, 104, 150, 153, 196, 197)*. As might be expected, there is a rush of literature about proposed research, discussions of scope and method, and exhortations as to the importance of the field. There is no unified theory (should or can there be one?). There are duplications and yet substantial gaps in the literature. Since practical situations vary so widely, and an underlying theory is lacking, practitioners seeking knowledge applicable to their immediate problem will often be baffled. Very often, the literature is useful only because it draws attention to an issue or because it develops methods of investigation which the practitioner can apply to his own particular puzzle.

In certain areas, at least, we already know a good deal more than most practitioners realize. We certainly know more than we apply. The field has attracted a flood of young, enterprising experimenters, many of whom come from planning or design and who are motivated to leap the classic gap between research and action. Furthermore, we inherit a substantial body of craft skill and common sense about the subject, which is, after all, rooted in everyday experience. This appendix cannot summarize what we know, because that knowledge is fairly extensive and because there is little useful theory by which it may be compressed. All that can be done here is to point to the areas in which substantial work has been done and then to the more glaring gaps (in terms of policy relevance rather than theoretical development). This brief discussion will be keyed to the research and reviews that are listed in the bibliography.

Sensing

The process of sensing and perceiving, particularly that of seeing, has been very extensively studied in psychology. The physiological process of sensation is fairly well understood, although the process of thinking is still a mystery. An understanding of perception is basic knowledge for anyone who deals with the perceived environment. Unfortunately, most work in perceptual psychology has been carried out in the laboratory, under controlled conditions, and where sensation is highly impoverished. It is difficult to apply those results to the confused, sequential, sensation-rich and socially contaminated perception of the everyday world. Only recently have some psychologists ventured into this confusing realm. More often, real-world experiments have been done by planners, designers, and geographers, whose principal interest is the environment. A few tests have been made of what people see on ordinary walks or drives and of how they organize those perceptions *(57, 73, 126)*. These efforts begin to inform us about what is remarked and how it is put together. More important, they have shown us how to discover this for ourselves in some particular, concrete situation not covered by previous testing. Recent work explores the correlations between the perception of models, movies, and drawings with that of the real places they represent, as a way of predicting the perception of proposed environments *(167, 171)*. There have been some tests of reactions to night lighting in the city which raise serious questions about present high-illumination standards *(97)*. A precise measure of the "visual intrusion" of any object in the eye's field of vision has been developed; this can be derived in the field, from photographs, or from plans, but its role in the complex act of perception is still unknown *(102)*.

Most of the relevant work has concentrated on vision, which is our dominant sense, especially when we interact with the environment. Hearing has received some attention, but outside the laboratory this has been focused almost exclusively on noise rather than on sound in general. Much of this work has treated noise primarily as a physical phenomenon, although these physical measures have been correlated with verbally expressed dissatisfactions. I am aware of only one study that treats the broader subject of the quality of sound, as perceived in the everyday world *(172)*. However, there has been some good recent work on the cumulative impact of ambient noise on hearing, on the health of the embryo, and on general physical health *(139)*.

There is interesting work on environmental perception by the handicapped. Some of the research deals with the special requirements of the blind and informs us of the latent capabilities of our nonvisual senses and how we may be influenced by the nonvisual environment in ways of which we are unconscious *(68)*. Work with people handicapped in other ways—the deaf and the crippled—is beginning to render similar insights. There are also some hints about the perception of the environment by psychotics or the mentally retarded *(162)*.

Parallel with the work on noise, there is substantial research on air pollution and its effects. This is less of a sensory phenomenon, of course, than a direct influence via body chemistry. Nevertheless, the visual and odorous consequences of air pollution are not negligible, and they are the influences that power the political drive toward clean air. Unfortunately, the field of "environmental quality" has tended to focus rather narrowly on measurable indices of undesirable, pervasive conditions of the physical environment, primarily the pollution of the air, land, and water. Attempts to create "environmental quality indices"—in the tradition of economic indices—by combining the levels of these various kinds of pollution are not only based on a maze of shaky assumptions (as discussed in Appendix 2) but exclude most of the universe of quality. To classify problems of the visible landscape as "visual pollution" not only is a misleading analogy but tends to restrict questions of quality to this same narrow range.

Finally, there is much craft knowledge about perception in the heads of practicing artists: painters, sculptors, architects, and landscape architects in particular *(61, 66, 81, 103, 109, 130, 143, 146, 155, 160)*. Some of this is transmitted in texts as part of the accumulated skill of the profession. Although not backed by scientific experiment, much of this knowledge is far from arbitrary, and it is extremely well fitted to practical application. In addition, it is useful in educating people to perceive in new ways, since it is the lore of the acute observer. But it also suffers from class and professional bias.

Environment and Behavior

Ergonomics (or human factors engineering) developed from efforts to improve the operation of military and industrial processes by adapting machines, working conditions, and the sequence of actions to human characteristics: body dimensions, muscular capability, sensitivity to noise, light, and temperature, the speed and accuracy of reactions, stress, fatigue, safety, inattention, disorientation, and the like *(95)*. Getting the best performance out of the human operator was the intent, and the studies focused on the immediate setting for some definite task. There are substantial data of this kind, including material on the capabilities of the handicapped.

A number of studies have recently been done on how larger settings seem to influence the visible behavior of people who are not narrowly task-oriented. Only a few years ago, such studies were a novelty; but now there is a substantial literature. Some of the most important work has been done by Robert Sommer *(169)* and by Roger Barker *(64)*, but there are numerous researchers in the field, and much unpublished work has been done by students preparing for careers in design. Without a strong unifying theory, this body of data is difficult to correlate, but some typical situations· have been repeatedly observed.

Perhaps the largest amount of work has been done on the use of the home and the local residential neighborhood, but there is also much material on behavior in hospitals, schools, and playgrounds *(132, 197)*. Studies of behavior in "total institutions," where people are kept in a single setting under a single control, are easier to accomplish and tend to have more striking results *(157)*. There is some interesting material on downtown streets and squares, as well as on fairs, museums, and exhibitions *(84, 89, 96, 136, 193)*. The activity of special groups has been followed, particularly children and the handicapped *(142, 173)*. A special subset of studies has concerned itself with crowding, or how behavior changes (and presumably deteriorates) as the density of occupation in a setting rises *(54)*. Some fascinating work has been done on the crowding of rats, but similar studies of human behavior are inconclusive. Work is only now beginning on the structure of behavior in time as well as in space: how people "spend their day" or how the use of a place fluctuates with hour and season *(132)*.

It is not easy to distinguish the influence of the environment alone on the stream of visible action, and indeed it is misleading to try to isolate it from the social setting. Even if we understand the linkage, should an environment then be designed to cause a predetermined behavioral outcome? Yet when one is using data observed on the spot, or from very similar cases with similar social contexts, and where it is also clear what people are trying to do in that place, behavioral data can be tremendously useful. Many interesting studies are wasted, sadly enough, because they are not communicated to designers or managers who are responsible for a setting, nor do they build up any accumulating body of knowledge. The investigation of how a place works, once occupied, should be a normal feature of environmental management and should have a built-in role in the future adaptation of that environment.

Roger Barker's concept of "behavior settings"—locations in which a physical setting and a repetitive pattern of behavior are consistently related to each other—is for a designer perhaps the most useful way of analyzing an inhabitated area. Constance Perin's "behavior circuits" could have equal usefulness *(148)*. Christopher Alexander has built a whole method of design around developing desirable "patterns" for behavior settings and then applying and modifying them under the control of actual users *(53)*.

Images
There has been a burst of work on mental images of the environment, based on a fusion of interests between environmental designers, geographers, and psychologists interested in cognition *(98)*. These studies use verbal descriptions, maps, models, and actual journeys in order to reveal the way a setting is identified and structured in someone's mind. The work has been replicated over the world, with a heavy concentration of studies in the United States and Great Britain *(55, 62, 70, 82, 90, 91, 92, 110, 111, 128, 153, 164, 168, 175, 176, 177, 178)*. One difficulty in this type of research is how to be sure one is actually getting at the structure carried inside someone else's head, and so there is continuing controversy over the correct methods to use. Another is how to go from the original static investigations to an understanding of how mental images develop with familiarity, age, or environmental change *(62, 90, 149)*. Still another difficulty is how these insights may be applied in environmental management. Many area

plans have used "image" jargon to justify designs that are, in fact, based on other motives, without bothering to analyze how the people in a place actually conceive of it or how the image differs by class and situation. Others have done image studies but have failed to apply them to policy questions. The whole concept of environmental images seems up to now to have had far more influence on research than on action. Nevertheless, I am convinced that studies of the images that people hold are as essential an element in planning their environment as are studies of how they actually act in a place. This conviction has been discussed at some length in the main body of this essay.

A particular subset of image studies is the idea of *territory*, originally a concept of animal behavior *(54, 83)*. Studies have been made of the degree of definition of the conceived neighborhood territory, or of the smaller territories that people establish whenever they act in a common space. This is an element of the environmental image which is relatively easy to elicit and which has clear implications for behavior, for social interaction, and even for the political process. Moreover, it coincides with the endemic planning ideal of the residential neighborhood. Recent studies show how to identify the pattern of conceived neighborhoods rather rapidly, even in complicated regions *(166)*. Some work has been done on the clues people use to recognize such territories or by which they infer the social status of their inhabitants, and so forth *(159)*.

Unfortunately, almost no research has been done on the environmental image of *time*: how people "tell time" by their setting; how it organizes the rhythm of their lives and symbolizes the past, present, and future *(131, 181)*. As noted earlier, this image may well be more significant to them than their image of space.

Preferences, Values, Meanings

There are many reports on environmental preferences, usually elicited by the straightforward method of asking people what they think of this or that feature of their environment, what they would prefer to have, how they would rank various alternatives, and so on. This can be useful material, particularly when it refers to judgments about the obvious features of places that people are actually experiencing. Interviews about housing satisfaction in Great Britain *(156)* and studies of "livability" in this country *(195)* have contributed a great deal to our understanding of environmental quality.

But ordinary questionnaires may impose an alien framework of values on people, or evoke only socially acceptable answers from them. Ideas of what one would like to have (unless these are conditions that one has already experienced) or a prediction about what one might do in the future are not very reliable. Straightforward preference interviews do not accurately gauge relative values, since they do not force people to make choices or to state under what constraints or at what costs they would prefer what they say. Therefore, more sophisticated ways of getting at preferences have been developed: using gaming, "personal constructs" (in which interviewees are required to set up their own dimensions of value before evaluating places), or questions about the costs people are willing to pay at the margin, or about the presumed preferences of their neighbors *(90, 135, 178, 188, 199)*. All of these methods help to penetrate the outermost layers of feeling, to evoke relative values, or to bypass stereotyped, socially correct, answers. Market values and actual histories of movement from one setting to another are, of course, objective reflections of these same internal values. But they are so contaminated by the actual choices available and by many other factors as to be difficult to interpret. Yet it is revealing to study the communication and creation of environmental preferences among social groups: how the idea of the ornamental front yard or the attraction to wild nature is transmitted; how values are attached to sea views or to ancient ruins *(86, 105)*.

It is possible to go to deeper levels of value and meaning by studying how a setting symbolizes fundamental feelings of security, identity, sexuality, and the like *(60, 78, 162)*. The material is fascinating but not always easy to apply. Perhaps the most useful source for these data is personal introspection, memories, and the references to place in novels and memoirs. Psychiatric methods may someday be useful here. However "unscientific," this information on the deep meaning of place will surely in the future be essential data for building a humane environment.

The Natural Environment

Because of management interests and resources, a large body of data has been collected on how people use and value "natural" landscapes: woodlands, parks, mountains, and so on *(163, 198, 199)*. The feelings of people about these natural settings have been probed, and their more practical comments about management, facilities, landscape style, and access have been collected. Some interesting work on the consistency of popular preferences for various types of landscape has been done *(163)*. In other studies, data from evaluations made in the field and from the inspection of photographs have been correlated *(79)*, the clues used have been analyzed, and some fairly stable preferences have been uncovered. Methods for identifying and recording landscape types as base data for management have been developed. There are substantial data on outdoor recreational preferences as evidenced by actual use.

In addition, there have been some intriguing studies of national or regional preferences for landscape style, in which social values and the state of the man-modified setting mutually affect each other over a long period, building up a stable, coherent, culturally specific concept of place value *(105, 125)*.

Communication and Learning

The most coherent data are in the areas already named: the act of sensing, environmental behavior, images, preferences, and the natural landscape. The work in other areas is much more scattered.

In regard to environmental communication, for example, there has been some work on the role of signs in the city *(121, 140)*. There has been much less on the clues that people use to infer who lives in a place or how it is used. There has been speculation about the need for complexity and even ambiguity in the environmental information that is presented, but very little empirical work, outside the laboratory, has been done *(154)*.

How learning and development are facilitated by a place is surely a fundamental issue, but again there is little beyond speculation here *(67, 72)*. Schools have been studied to see how they facilitate or discourage school learning, but this is straightforward behavioral observation, which does not penetrate very far into how places are occasions for growth. "Environmental education" takes people out into the world to teach them about the (primarily natural) environment, and its methods give us clues about the quality of a setting which makes it a good teaching device *(93)*. The work of Robin Moore with children is as close to building a learning environment as we have come *(141)*, or we might add the way in which the Ecologue project employed self-administered use and image studies to encourage people to learn about their relations with the world *(71)*. Piaget did the classic work on the development of intelligence in children, but this was done in the laboratory, with very simple objects *(149)*. An understanding of how people change and grow as a result of their interaction with their environment, which might lead to the building of true learning places, is one of the basic research tasks ahead of us.

Gaps

Indeed, although we know much more than we act upon, there are numerous gaps in our knowledge of the sensory environment. It may be worth the space to list some of them here:
- The sensory requirements of special groups in the population: the young, old, handicapped, and so on.

- How environmental values among various groups are changing, or may be expected to change. How they are created and communicated.
- The role of smell and other "subordinate" senses.
- The role of sensory quality in low-resource situations: squatter settlements, and other such places.
- The act of perception in the midst of complexity: the role of kinesthesia, of ambiguity.
- The use and image of the workplace by the worker (in contrast to the "time and motion" and "human factors" studies used to speed up production).
- Sensory programming: how to specify the desired sense of a setting as a guide to its design and management.
- Participatory methods in sensory design and programming.
- The image of time and change.
- The deep symbolism of place.
- Methods for predicting the sensory qualities of any proposal.
- Ways of storing and manipulating sensory representations and of developing environmental indices.
- Developing new environmental prototypes and the processes for doing so, through a direct coupling of research and action.
- Environment as a stimulus and occasion for learning: how it may encourage people to develop to their full potential.

Given the numerous gaps, as well as the lack of unifying theory, the practitioner often finds that the most useful feature of present research is not its substantive content. It is valuable, in the first place, because it has pointed out a whole series of issues that he cannot now ignore. Second, it has developed new methods that he can use himself to illuminate his own particular problem. Naturally, he is most interested in those methods which are simple and rapid enough to use even while designing a place under the pressure of decision. Such techniques have been described elsewhere in this essay, particularly in Appendix 2. In general, and in addition to the familiar field surveys of the "objective" form of the sensory environment, they can be reduced to a few quite straightforward methods: the on-site observation of behavior; interviews with sample users as to their use, image, and preferences in regard to an existing known place; and the observation of activity traces, signs, and other "unobtrusive measures" in the field, which are the significant clues as to how people actually use and value their places. In this work, tape recorders, still and motion cameras, videotape, and, of course, the ancient, sympathetic human eye and ear turn out to be the primary equipment.

Appendix 4: Some Detailed, but Hypothetical, Examples of Regional Studies for Sensory Quality

The main text has laid out a long series of possible objectives and types of regional action for sensory quality in the section called "What For?" These were no more than topic headings. Let us sketch a few examples in more detail. They may, however, still seem somewhat mysterious, for they are not actual proposals, under real constraints, for some specific place, whose residents have particular goals and priorities.

Nevertheless, it seems useful to try to outline some hypothetical cases—at least in an appendix that the reader is free to skip over. I have arbitrarily chosen four possible sensory issues, which range from familiar and definite actions to more exotic and indefinite ones. In each case, I have pointed out the basis for the particular policy, the surveys and analyses that might be required, the public actions that are possible, and the various tests and techniques involved. In addition, I have suggested the likely costs, constraints, and conflicts that will appear and have given some idea of the financial, political, ·and administrative implementation required. These discussions are purely hypothetical and suggestive.

Maintaining Distant Views

Let us begin with a policy that is familiar: the conservation of existing panoramic and distant views and the creation of new ones, (a topic listed under "Sensing and Acting"). Such views are often considered to be one of the more characteristic and cherished features of a region *(120)*, and a public policy for their conservation can be based on a wide consensus *(21)*. Particular panoramas may have deep symbolic meaning, as evidenced in histories, guidebooks, novels, paintings, memoirs, and references in the media. The regional agency may refer to political battles that have erupted when views were threatened and to the economic reflection of those values, which is revealed by the variation in real estate prices and rents. Reference can also be made to the physiology of the eye, which "rests" on distant landscapes, and to the psychological satisfactions of orientation, identity, and inclusive panoramas. The agency may turn to sample interviews, in order to gauge the depth and consistency of the preference for views. It may also investigate the actual frequency of use of panoramic points by residents and visitors.

A survey of the major existing public views in the region would be a natural next step, including those from the key panoramic viewpoints and from the main public corridors *(43)*. The extent and nature of these views would be mapped, along with the dominant features seen, and all of this would be described in photographs or sketches. Objects that blocked, or threatened to block, those views would be noted. Fine potential views would also be mapped, with the clearance or access needed to realize them. Viewing points should include the important indoor locations that are accessible to the general public. Attempts might be made to go beyond the mapping of these dominant views in order to measure, or at least to describe, how various areas of the region have a greater or lesser frequency of outward view. By noting the frequency of distant (or even midrange) views in sample areas, a classification of districts by "eye range" might be attempted. Recent history would certainly be reviewed in order to understand the way in which existing development processes and public rules act to enhance or destroy the public views.

Parallel studies must also be made of the degree to which diverse types of residents are aware of distant views and whether they value them or go out of their way to enjoy them. One would want to find out what particular views are most valued, and in what circumstances: while traveling, at leisure, at home, or at work. Some check might be made of the reference to local views in newspapers, novels, paintings, guidebooks, political controversies, and so on.

On the basis of this information, a great number of public actions are possible. Without a real situation to restrain me, or to indicate priorities, I shall simply list them. The public agency may impose particular "view easements," whether through special development regulations (see Fig. 13) or by purchase (145). These easements can radiate from a point or run along some important line of transportation or natural edge, such as a coastline. View easements may be generalized into broad rules of height, bulk, and plant cover, which will maintain views along a road, or a seacoast, or from the hills. Height limits may be graded upward from a coastline or toward hillcrests to allow the structures behind to "look over" the ones in front. "Visual penetration" rules may be enforced in order to allow intermittent views of the sea or from hilltops, rules that require a certain frequency of openings in planting and fences as well as buildings (6).

In reverse, regulations may be placed on the critical points to be seen—preventing the construction of buildings (or high buildings) on important visual crests or promontories, for example. Crucial skylines, landmarks, frontages, or visual bowls (that is, spatial basins within which most points are intervisible) may be defined, which are not to be visibly disturbed.

More general programmatic rules may be considered: the requirement of visual "holes," or even of public viewing stations, in any new buildings erected in dense areas, for example, or a requirement that any blockage of an existing view must be compen-

sated by the opening of a new one. There could be a general policy—
to be carried out by regulations or by public construction—that
every important public space or road should have at least one view
out toward some specified key symbolic feature. Sensory programs
for new development at key locations can specify the views to be
retained and the new ones to be developed. Density bonuses might
be granted for structures or land clearances that enhance the view.

Direct public actions are also possible: new panoramic viewpoints can be constructed, or roads and transit lines can be sited to
develop the views that can be seen from them. Artificial lighting
can be used to enhance the view at night. All these ideas can be
recorded and coordinated in a framework plan that locates the
major viewpoints, corridors, and view fields, specifies their desired
quality, and shows what is to be saved and what created. It may
also delineate the "shut-in" areas that are judged substandard in
frequency and quality of outward views, the key terrains that
dominate what is seen and are therefore most sensitive to change
(see Fig. 34), and the visual compartments that are relatively isolated from outward sight and can thus be modified without disturbing any regional panoramas (see Fig. 36).

The regional agency may also consider whether there is any legal
means of conferring "view rights" on property owners or communities, that is, whether an existing development or neighborhood with a fine view can claim compensation from any new development that blocks that view, giving them cause for court action or a basis for negotiation with the builder of the new project.
Clearly, much thought would have to be given to how that right
could be defined, how it would interact with existing property
rights, and what its social consequences might be if widely applied.

In a more modest way, the agency might issue design guidelines
or handbooks on how to build without blocking the view, or even
how to enhance the view by new construction. Advisory design
review in critical areas, with publicized sketches showing the

superposition of some proposal on the existing view, can be quite effective. In a more dramatic way, the agency might require a full-scale, on-site mock-up of the outline of any major new structure at some critical point—as by means of a light framework, or by cables of the proposed height, held aloft by balloons, at the proposed building corners.

Such actions may have widespread support, and their aim is familiar. They generate some predictable conflicts. There will often be an acute confrontation with developers, whose right to build at a location in the form and intensity desirable to them is threatened *(21)*. Often, the very building that blocks a view does so in order to gain the maximum economic advantage from that same view for itself. There is an overt struggle between the public and the private appropriation of a resource whose ownership has not been clearly defined but which has up to then been enjoyed without conflict or without a realization of who was taking what from whom.

In addition to this direct competition, view regulations are sure to increase the delays and complexities in the construction approval process and may at times make it awkward to develop any building of reasonable size or regularity of shape. The public access to a new viewpoint may be a serious intrusion on privacy or an invitation to vandalism and trespass. Such secondary costs must be foreseen and accounted for.

Other problems can arise. View protection and enhancement may increase the inequalities of sense in the region, since they will apply most frequently to those areas with the best potential views, which are most likely already occupied by the more affluent people. Thus we would stress the importance of focusing on heavily frequented public viewpoints and corridors, and of considering comparative, areawide measures of "eye range."

Finally, it may turn out that, while a view has been opened up, what is viewed from it is beyond control and rapidly deteriorates.

It is much easier to maintain a small public point from which to look out or an aerial opening than it is to monitor broad stretches of visible ground. Luckily, the thing seen is so often an "eternal" object, like a mountain or the sea, or it is so complex and so distant, like the far view of a city center, that it maintains its attraction through a myriad of uncontrolled changes.

In general, the protection of important views is likely to be an objective that is widely understood and agreed upon, and the principal difficulty in implementing such a policy will be the opposition of the private development interest. Political support for these measures, as is so often true in sensory issues, is likely to be diffuse, ill-organized, and inattentive. Yet if guided and given clear evidence of what is at stake, this support can be decisive. The stoppage of some "inevitable" projects in Jerusalem *(21)*, the controversy over high-rise buildings in downtown San Francisco *(43)*, and the sweeping height limits imposed by referendum in San Diego are just a few examples of the latent power in this issue (see Fig. 56).

The financial costs of view protection are relatively small, except when they appear as restraints on private development or when it becomes necessary to purchase a view easement. Direct public costs are liable to be absorbed as charges on the general funds or will be an inextricable part of the costs of constructing, say, a public highway. Some indirect public costs resulting from increased density may appear if view incentives are used. Raising funds by charging people for the use of panoramic view points seems a dubious tactic. It might be possible to allow developers to block existing views on payment of a fee, which would go into a fund for the purchase of new public view easements. But in many cases, this may simply not be worth the trouble.

Analyses and policies for controlling the public view will call a number of new (and old) techniques into play. Among them are the mapping of view platforms and view fields; the graphic descrip-

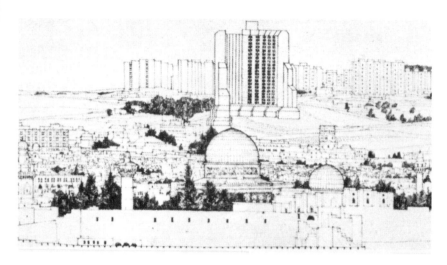

HIGH, WIDE AND...

The latest planning controversy in Jerusalem centres on a proposal for a high-rise hotel on the lower slope of Mount Scopus which, its critics say, would change the character of the historic hill and become the dominant element in the environs of the Old City. The hotel architects say the building would enrich the skyline. **ABRAHAM RABINOVICH reports.**

56 The newspaper publication of this unauthorized drawing, showing the visual effect of a proposed hotel on the setting of old Jerusalem, raised such widespread opposition that the project was canceled.

tion of views, and the simulation of changes in them; the use of composite panoramic photos, fish-eye cameras, and "visual intrusion" grids *(112, 123)*; computer systems for delineating view fields; diagrams of intervisibility, view access, and the relative "eye range" of different areas; techniques for specifying view performance in sensory programs and framework designs; interview protocols for uncovering citizen knowledge and values about viewing; and experiments with full-scale on-site simulation, with guided view tours for educational purposes, or with the creation of lighted spectacles in the landscape to be seen from the major viewpoints.

This is no new issue, incidentally. To quote a provision from the Code of Justinian (538 A.D.):

Nov. 63. In this our royal city one of the most pleasing amenities is the view of the sea; and to preserve it we enacted that no building should be erected within 100 feet of the sea front. This law has been circumvented by certain individuals. They first put up buildings conforming with this law; then put up in front of them awnings which cut off the sea view without breaking the law; next put up a building inside the awning; and finally remove the awning. Anyone who offends in this way must be made to demolish the building he has put up and further pay a fine of ten pounds of gold.

A few years later, an addition was made to this law:

165. The law [Nov. 63] that no building must be erected within 100 feet of the sea to obstruct the sea view applies to the side view as well as the front. *(186)*

View regulation has familiar problems!

Providing Public Shelter

If view regulation is a direct and familiar action under the head of sensory quality, the provision of public shelter is an equally direct but perhaps less familiar object of general policy, although scattered public shelters have frequently been built. In this case, the object is to increase the comfort, healthfulness, and convenience of a city by protecting its inhabitants from rain, snow, hot sun, cold, and strong winds. The unpleasantness of the urban microclimate is one of the most frequent of all citizen complaints, but very little is done to mitigate it.

Sheltering is not difficult to justify, and there are likely to be few interests directly opposed to it. Controversy is more likely to center on its cost and whether that cost is justified. Actions can be based on arguments of citizens whose health is impaired by exposure, on the widely felt discomfort of rain and wind and wet feet, and on the way in which bad weather restricts the movements of the young, the elderly, and the handicapped. The economic attractiveness of covered shopping malls, as well as the effects of inclement weather on public transit, absenteeism at work, and commercial sales, can be cited.

To put policy on a sound footing, surveys of the location and use of existing shelter will be required—not only of intentional structures such as arcades and bus shelters but also of the rainy-day use of doorways, umbrellas, and awnings, and observations of where people stand in heavy wind. Analyses of the local incidence of precipitation, wind, and temperature extremes will be needed, and a sampling of the way in which microclimates vary in the region, including how they are affected by surrounding structures and cover, will be required. These conditions must then be compared to known data on human tolerances and comfort ranges.

To justify the construction of a shelter, people would be interviewed, particularly in bad weather, and their actions photographed. Data would also be required on pedestrian densities in various areas, the time spent in waiting outdoors, and on such special needs as the necessary movements of the aged and handicapped. Information would also be wanted on the cost and maintenance of various protective structures and about any special

problems they raise, such as encouraging criminal activity and vandalism. Police and public maintenance crews should be interviewed
in regard to this aspect.

Given these motives and data, there are many actions that a regional or city agency might take with respect to sheltering. It
might draw up an areawide plan for shelters, public and private,
including overhead shelters, windscreens, and heated enclosures
and comprising both point shelters where people congregate
and continuous shelters (arcades, malls, tunnels, and skyways)
where there is heavy pedestrian flow. This would be a framework
plan of location and general characteristics, and there would be a
set of program requirements for typical situations. It would indicate the facilities to be provided privately, whether by incentive or
regulation, and those to be furnished by public agencies, including
budgets, timing, and the responsibility for construction and for
maintenance. This is a familiar type of facilities plan in an operational form. It would be based on explicit standards of how frequently shelter should occur, depending on pedestrian density,
waiting times, and microclimate, and under what conditions continuous arcades were desirable.

Detailed performance standards for shelters would then be developed: the degree of weather protection; when enclosure, cooling,
or heating is needed; the required visibility into and out of them;
seating, telephones, floor, and lighting needs; qualities of perma-
nence and maintenance; entrances, dimensions, and capacities; the
fit into the existing context; and similar matters.

Rules might be set for private buildings in regard to awnings,
marquees, inset doorways, wind fences, public seats, and canopies
along building fronts, arcades in parking lots, the connection of
interior malls to the public streets, and the prevention of wind
focusing or of reflected glare. In some areas there might be density
incentives for providing public shelter, or fees imposed on buildings that worsen the microclimate. Specific shelter programs might

be part of the conditions imposed on large new developments. Required arcade lines could be mapped, or private builders might be allowed to build over the public sidewalks, if they provided a specified arcade at street level.

Design guidelines might be prepared on how to plan shelters of various kinds, as well as other features that have a sheltering potential, such as doorways and fences. Particular problems could be addressed: how to build arcades along an existing commercial frontage of mixed age, how shelters might cross vehicular streets, how to build temporary or movable shelters, or how to take advantage of existing structures with shelter potential, such as elevated highways, ruined buildings, or old walls. A prototype shelter might be erected and tested for its usefulness.

The agency might well consider how to encourage local communities to build their own shelter systems—whether by technical assistance, by the provision of parts and materials, or by subsidy. Clearly, the issues of shelter ownership and maintenance and the problems of preventing crime and vandalism would have to be addressed.

It is not very likely that direct combat will arise over these measures. A major issue will be cost—first cost and maintenance—and whether that is justified as a public or a private charge. Major attention in the agency would therefore be given to ways of reducing cost, ways of raising necessary funds, and ways of finding a workable consensus as to what levels of use will justify given levels of cost. Of course, existing shelters that are rarely used may be an embarrassment.

There may well be secondary issues, however. There can be fears of vandalism, reduced safety in enclosed or sheltered places, or the possible attraction of "vagrants." (Not an uncommon thorn in the side of environmental quality is that the very success of an improvement may attract too many of what others judge to be the "wrong people.") Technical problems can arise, such as an interference with deliveries, solid waste disposal, or emergency vehicles. It may be quite difficult to add shelter to existing heavily built-up areas and equally puzzling to find means for sheltering people in new, sprawling low-density commercial strips *(174)*. Some costs will be added to new private development, when building owners are no longer allowed to dump heat, reflect glare, or channel wind into public spaces. Predicting microclimate effects will be a further drag on project completions, and shelter performance costs must be added to project costs. So clear are the advantages, however—at least at moderate to high densities—that these are not the major obstacles. Public construction cost, maintenance, and policing look like the key difficulties.

Thus the agency will search for means of financing these structures: as a regular part of building public ways (just as sidewalks are today), as part of building a transit system (bus shelters belong with terminals, vehicles, and trackage), by associations of local merchants, by development rules and incentives, or even by the subscription and labor of local neighborhoods. It will be important to insert the sheltering function as a normal part of line agency construction and maintenance: in public works departments, transit agencies, park boards, and police.

Since shelters are relatively small physical structures, the techniques involved in this work are primarily those of architecture and engineering. But interviews and behavioral observation, as well as ways of representing and predicting the urban microclimate, are also important.

Conserving Local History

A policy for conserving the historical continuity of ordinary local areas will be a somewhat less familiar idea than view control or public shelter. I am referring, not to historic preservation in the classic sense, which is devoted to the restoration and protection of outstanding ancient buildings, but to a policy of ensuring that *every* part of a region should express its continuity with the past, however commonplace. Such a policy would be founded on present knowledge of the psychology of memory and identity, and of its importance for human well-being and coherent function *(131)*. This central foundation can be elaborated by the expression of citizens' attachment to their localities and their local histories, and by recounting the cases of political resistance to total clearance and renewal. The growing power of the preservation movement can be cited, especially now that it is moving into the local residential neighborhoods. The commercial values of nostalgia can be touched upon. It may also be argued that a general, areawide conservation and explanation of the past will increase the knowledge, and pleasure, and perhaps even the political cohesion of regional residents.

An analysis of this issue would clearly begin with a compilation of the known history of the region—its topographic history in particular. Special emphasis would be given to the histories of small local areas and of the diverse populations. Graphic material on the region's history would be put together, covering as much of the region as possible. As a contrast, sample interviews would be used to gauge citizen awareness of, and interest in, local history. "Oral history" would be gathered, or its collection stimulated.

Along with this collection of materials, it would be necessary to investigate and illustrate the degree to which the existing landscape preserves traces of the past and how legible those traces are. The role of public rules and private development in saving or erasing those traces would have to be analyzed. Attitudes toward history among the key decision makers would also be of interest.

Historic conservation has almost always been a case-by-case (or district-by-district) affair. If regionwide action is thought to be desirable, then a large number of new public actions become possible. Among these possibilities might be a series of conditions to be met by any new development that replaces some former occupancy: for a given number of years, the new structures or sites must preserve and display fragments of the old buildings, landscaping, or site furniture; they must mark out the traces of former locations, shapes, and circulation lines; or they must display a graphic and verbal description of the former occupation. In critical zones, general rules of this kind might be transmuted into a specific program for new development, specifying what to save and what to express. The next step, in ascending order of precision and rigidity, is to specify just what objects must be preserved entirely. This is the familiar historical landmark procedure. For larger areas, rules of scale or restraints on material might be imposed—all designed to recall the previous use and to tie new buildings harmoniously into their older context.

A regional archive on environments and environmental behavior might be established, where the characteristics of typical places about to disappear were systematically recorded, stored, and made available for future study—in the form of maps, site and architectural drawings, photographs, movies of street action, tapes of street noises, videotape interviews, and so on. It might be a requirement that any environmental renewal over a certain scale must contribute a record of what it is replacing to that archive, in some prescribed form.

Localities could be encouraged to analyze the sense of continuity among their own citizenry, to investigate their own history and the environmental traces it has left behind. They could make local plans for conservation, mark out the location and scale of former buildings and activities, post old views and descriptions at the corresponding spots, display photographs of former local residents, arrange the reenactment of local events, set up their own archives, and even appoint a local conservator. With suitable safeguards, localities might be empowered to dedicate permanent local memorials, plant commemorative trees and stones, commemorate local occasions, births, and deaths, perhaps even permit local burials.

The intent would be not simply to recover and express the past but to memorialize living local history as it occurs.

Furthermore, a regional agency can delineate areas that are comparatively impoverished in historic traces, develop design guides on how to maintain historic continuity in new development without impairing present function, and encourage widespread public and semipublic education in environmental history. Tours, seminars, and field workshops can be organized. Archaeological games can be played, and much of this information be communicated through the newspapers, radio, and television.

Most probably, these activities would not be directly opposed as being improper; they are more likely to be questioned as to their relative importance. Opponents might also ask whether these activities are more properly the concern of specialized private groups, or whether they should be confined to the outstanding, "truly historic" places. While the direct costs of this kind of regional historic preservation are not large (in contrast to the classic retention and renovation of entire buildings or areas), still the amount of staff energy demanded could well come under political fire. Moreover, new development, while not blocked or made less profitable, would have to contend with some new restrictions and procedures. Thus the value of local history must be carefully assessed, and the political backing of neighborhoods, ethnic groups, and conservationists must be assembled.

Secondary conflicts may arise with newcomers, "modernists," or others who are relatively indifferent to a sense of history, or even actively opposed to its expression. In areas occupied by a mixture of groups, there may be sharper conflicts over *whose* history is to be saved, and which version of past events is correct. There may be some painful lessons in pluralistic tolerance to learn.

In addition, there can be technical problems: health issues in regard to local burials as a substitute for our customary disposal in segregated, outlying cemeteries; questions about the maintenance of historic traces; or the possibility of an awkward cumulative "littering" of the landscape, as it builds up historic depth.

While the direct costs are small, they are not zero. Some of them can be taken up by historical societies and local groups. Others will be added to the cost of new development. There may be federal or foundation grants available for special activities, such as the environmental archive, or an oral history, or a local reenactment of an event. There may well be a pool of enthusiastic volunteer labor that can be tapped, and some of the work can be carried out in the schools. Agency staff resources are likely to be a continuing problem, however, without consistent political backing. It seems unlikely that any of these costs could easily be raised by user fees.

Most of the techniques to be used would be familiar ones: historic maps and views, maps and photographs of existing traces, comparative views, historic and descriptive markers, and so on. The most interesting new technical problem is that of creating a systematic environmental archive, recording former locations, forms, activities, sounds, and memories of places distributed over the entire region, yet in a compact and retrievable way that can continue to receive new records. Clearly, many media would have to be employed: verbal, graphic, and auditory, in static and dynamic forms. The systematic filing and compressed storage of such heterogeneous material would be no simple problem.

Encouraging Rooted Information

As the final example, I have chosen a still less familiar issue; but, like the immediately previous one, it is concerned with symbolic communication. This would be a policy that encouraged the display of rooted information and in contrast discouraged unrooted displays. By "rooted" information I mean communications that speak directly of the place itself and of its associations: names, addresses, services provided at that place, products manufactured or distributed there, local events, values and ideas of residents and workers, and so on *(140)*. Crosses on churches, personal political statements on houses, and beer signs on taverns are "rooted" signs. Billboards and the normal election posters are "unrooted" signs. The proliferation of advertising signs is a common criticism of the American landscape. But on inquiry, we find that most of the signs on stores and on public buildings have a very important informative function *(2)*. They tell us where things are and what or who is available there. Unrooted signs do not have this key environmental function. Thus the visual aggression of the billboard is very widely disliked.

The relative suppression of unrooted displays may be justified as preventing competition with rooted signs and the signs of public control, both of which presumably have a higher priority. Billboards and posters are unrelated to the landscape and are most often the prime visual despoilers of it. They are private advertising for profit, yet they use a public medium without charge: the visual corridor of the right of way. Unlike the advertising in a newspaper or on television, they cannot easily be turned off or set aside. Numerous public investigations have exposed a widespread dislike of unrooted signs, while shop signs arouse mixed feelings or are perhaps appreciated, although their form and scale may be criticized. In contrast, the public agency may encourage rooted information (given proper controls on its location and form) on the grounds of increasing citizen knowledge of their city and of improving orientation and access.

Since the concern is with all the means by which information is transmitted in the landscape, the first necessity is a careful survey of just how this occurs: the various types of transmissions, their typical location and relative density, the ways in which they interfere with each other or with other features of the landscape, their relative legibility, how they are mounted or carried, and the distinctions between rooted and unrooted, explicit and implicit, public and private, intended and unintended, obtrusive and unobtrusive (see Fig. 43). In an extensive region, this is a complex subject, and a regional survey is likely to be confined to distinguishing and locating the principal types of signs and sign contexts, making sample counts as a basis for estimates of quantity, and perhaps completing a schematic mapping of the various types *(2)*. In order to illustrate the typical kinds of signs and sign contexts, a photographic survey of sample areas will also be necessary. This will be very useful later, when estimating the impact of various policies.

Depending on perceived problems, the survey may go into greater detail on certain issues, such as the visibility of traffic control signs, or of street signs and building addresses, the clarity of general orientation information, the posting of transit schedules or notices about when services are open, the message content of billboards and posters, the relation of signs to parks or to residential areas, or the use of light and motion.

On-street interviews could be conducted to see how citizens use and feel about various kinds of signs in various contexts. If there was a proposal to insert new kinds of information into the landscape—such as bus schedules or ecological descriptions—a few might be put up experimentally to check their use. On the other hand, it would be necessary to become familiar with the processes by which information comes to be displayed: the economics of the various sectors of the sign industry, the economic values of signs to their clients, the way decisions about public signs are made, existing regulations and how they are administered, and so on.

Once more, there are a number of actions that the regional agency may choose to take. The most familiar action is that of regulation: to forbid unrooted signs outright or to confine them to special zones, such as in industrial areas or along expressways, where they compete with little rooted information, are less likely to deflect driver attention when it is needed elsewhere, and are less likely to deface other features of the landscape. Or there may simply be rules as to size, location, and the use of light and motion in order to reduce the dominance of the unrooted symbols. A more radical action would be to charge a fee for use of the public visual air space by unrooted signs, depending on their size, length of message, distance from which they are visible, and numbers of persons exposed to them. Receipts could be devoted to the purchase of visual easements, or to the improvement of rooted information, or to other public purposes.

The obverse of these restrictive policies is the encouragement of desirable rooted signs. Building addresses are commonly required. Names, type of service, and hours of opening might also be asked of all locations accessible to the public. Rooted information might become an expected element of all public works and services: posted transit routes and schedules (and even signals of the imminent arrival of vehicles), legible street signs, public clocks, weather data, general orientation information, descriptions of local history and ecology, explanations of public works in process, and so on. Special public information centers might be put up at points of heavy use (2). There could be incentives (of sign location, size, or just prestige) given for desirable rooted information posted by private agencies. "Transparencies," which would let people on the sidewalk see what was happening inside a building or enclosed area, would be encouraged. Sensory programs for new development could include stipulations about the rooted information that must be displayed.

Associated with these measures, of course, there would be regulations or recommendations on the size, location, and form of signs, which would be designed to prevent sign interference, to liberate captive attention, or to prevent the dominance of high-priority information by less desirable intrusions. The staff of an agency might prepare a handbook on sign design, dealing with clarity, harmony, rootedness, relevance, and congruence (or the way in which the form of a sign fits the form of the idea being conveyed—on the assumption that an area symbol is desirable for an area regulation, for example). Seminars with sign designers, sign manufacturers, and sign users might be conducted.

Places that were substandard in regard to environmental information would be publicly identified, and places that were particularly informative might be given some public recognition. Area tours could be organized. Along major roads, there might even be local broadcasts, somewhat like the automated tours in museums, that would allow drivers to tune in and to hear a running commentary on the area they were passing through.

The management of environmental information will be full of controversy, since many crosscutting interests are at stake here. The principal conflict will be with the sign industry itself, whose basic livelihood is involved. However, the industry has many separate segments, which are more or less involved with unrooted signing. Billboards, for example, are quasi-monopolies at the national scale, while posters are produced by small local shops. Electric signs are manufactured by large companies, selling nationally, and they are highly competitive. And there are many other examples. Shops and other businesses have quite varied sign needs, but so do many nonprofit institutions. Public support for sign control is widespread but diffuse, and it must be focused. The issue is complex and can generate great heat on both sides. The agency responsible for managing environmental information must understand the interests involved quite thoroughly before it ventures to act. The administrative load in detailed sign regulation can be substantial, and so can the erection and maintenance of widespread public rooted signing. There are familiar technical difficulties, such as the control of temporary signs, moving signs, aerial signs, audible signs, street decorations, and the personal displays in residential areas.

More fundamental issues are also involved, since information is linked to power. The revelation of some rooted information

("What goes on here?") may be resisted as invasion of privacy. On the other hand, the suppression of unrooted information, particularly of election posters, will be seen as an infringement of free speech. For many local—or poor—political candidates, the display of outdoor posters may be one of the few publicity means available. Thus special concessions may have to be made at election times. (The removal of old election posters—indeed of temporary signs in general—is always a headache, however.) Even the introduction of innocuous ecological information at a site may be seen, by some, as "littering" or "defacing" the landscape. A public policy must thread its way through this maze of opposition. Open public debate between all the interests involved is essential.

Nevertheless, the control and the encouragement of signs, both as information sources and as esthetic objects, are relatively inexpensive and rapid ways of improving the environment. These policies have very wide public support, and much of the opposition is quite divided in its interests and is thus open to political realignment. Moreover, there are potential public revenues here in the form of fees for the use of the public visual field.

The analytical techniques involved are standard ones: field surveys, mappings, continuous photographic elevations for record purposes, sign and word counts, visibility analyses, measurements of luminance, studies of lettering legibility, photographic simulations of sign changes, street interviews, and so on.

Out of all the issues that might be taken up by a regional agency, I have chosen only four examples, surely a small portion of the set listed in the section "What For?"—itself an incomplete list but containing 90 topics. This sample hypothetical elaboration may give the reader a better sense of the depth and complexity of regional sense quality and of the pressing need to use a selective strategy when operating upon it.

Bibliographies

Key
*Important example or source.
[see 14] : Also see reference number 14.
[fig. 42] : Figure 42 is taken from this reference.
[cited 37, 72] : This reference is cited on pp. 37 and 72 of text.

A Bibliography of Examples

*1. Appleyard, D., and Lynch, K., *Temporary Paradise? A Look at the Special Landscape of the San Diego Region*, and its technical appendix, for the Planning Department, San Diego, Calif., 1974. [figs. 1, 2, 14; cited 58, 83, 112]

2. Ashley, Myer, Smith, Inc., *City Signs and Lights*. A project by Signs/Lights/Boston, January 1971. [cited 30, 34, 193, 194, 195]

*3. Barnett, J., *Urban Design as Public Policy*. Architectural Record Books, New York, 1974. [see 27, 35; fig. 13; cited 47, 83]

4. Barton-Aschman Associates, *Organizing for Better Urban Design in Minneapolis*, for Minneapolis Planning Commission. [see 29, 48; cited 82]

5. Boston Redevelopment Authority, *Downtown Design and Development Study*. Boston, 1969.

6. California Coastal Zone Conservation Commission, *Appearance and Design*, June 1974; North Central Coast Regional Commission, *Policies: Appearance and Design*, July 1974; and South Coast Regional Commission, *Appearance and Design in the South Coast Region*, September 1974. [see 34; cited 71, 83, 179]

*7. Carney, W., *Where We Stand: A Report on Leverett's Planning Process*. Leverett Conservation Commission and Planning Board, Leverett, Mass., November 1973. [cited 27, 35, 111]

8. Cerasi, M., *Valori ambientali del comprensorio Lodigiano*, Instituto Lombardo per gli Studi Economici e Sociali, Milan, July 1967. [cited 85]

9. Cerasi, M., *Analisi e progrettazione dell'ambiente: Uno studio per la valle del Ticino*, Ente provinciale per il turismo di Milano, 1970. [see 17, 52; cited 71, 85]

10. Commission Intercommunale d'Urbanisme, *Plan Directeur de la Region Lausannoise, Analyse des Sites et Aspects Pratiques de Leur Protection*, Lausanne, Switzerland, 1970. [figs. 11, 35; cited 71, 85]

11. Dallas Department of Urban Planning, *The Visual Form of Dallas*, Dallas, Tex., ca. 1974. [see 20, 23, 24, 28, 31, 33, 39, 43]

12. DeCarlo, G., *Urbino*, Marsilio, Padova, 1966. English ed.: Cambridge, Mass., 1970.

13. Detroit City Planning Commission, *Inner City Design Resources*, Detroit, 1969. [cited 5, 81]

*14. Detroit City Planning Commission, *Detroit 1990: An Urban Design Concept for the Inner City*, Detroit, 1970. [see 42; fig. 12; cited 81]

15. Federal Highway Administration, *Manual, National Scenic Highway Study*, 1974. [see 19, 22, 38, 47]

16. Fines, K. D., "Landscape Evaluations: A Research Project in East Sussex," *Regional Studies*, March 1968. [see 18, 36, 41, 44, 49, 50; cited 71, 84]

17. Greater London Council, Department of Architecture and Civic Design, *Thames-side Environmental Assessment*, London, March 1968. [see 9, 52; fig. 53; cited 84, 115]

*18. Jacobs, P., "The Landscape Image," *Town Planning Review*, April 1975. [see 16, 36, 41, 44, 49, 50; cited 6, 71, 81, 84]

19. Jones and Jones, *Scenic and Recreational Highway Study*, for the Legislative Transportation Committee, State of Washington, Seattle, 1974. [see 15, 22, 38, 47; fig. 52; cited 6, 71, 84, 99, 115]

20. Kansas City Planning Department, *Measuring the Visual Environment*, CRP Technical Report No. 11, Kansas City, Mo., 1967. [see 11, 23, 24, 28, 31, 33, 39, 43; cited 5]

*21. Kutcher, A., *The New Jerusalem: Planning and Politics*, MIT Press, Cambridge, Mass., 1975. [figs. 8, 17, 18, 33, 36, 37, 55, 57; cited 19, 71, 85, 178, 181, 182]

22. Lewis, P., "Quality Corridors for Wisconsin," *Landscape*, Spring 1966. [see 15, 22, 38, 47; cited 84, 99]

23. Los Angeles City Planning Commission, *The Visual Environment of Los Angeles*, Los Angeles, Calif., April 1971. [see 11, 20, 24, 28, 31, 33, 39, 43; figs. 6, 47; cited 5, 82]

*24. Lynch, K., *Visual Analysis*, Community Renewal Program, Brookline, Mass., September 1965. [see 11, 20, 23, 28, 31, 33, 39, 43; figs. 21, 22, 48, 49; cited 81]

25. MacManus, F., and G. Cullen, *Tenterden Explored*, Kent County Council, Maidstone, Kent, England, 1967. [cited 85]

26. Marans, R. W., *A Manual on the Development of an Environmental Study for Design Resources*, Detroit Regional Transportation and Land Use Study, July 1967.

27. Markus, M., and J. West, "Urban Design Through Zoning," *Planner's Notebook*, Vol. 2, No. 5 (October 1972), American Institute of Planners. [see 3, 35; cited 83]

28. Melting, A., *Description and Analysis of the Visual Form of Rye*, four vols., mimeo., Rye, N.Y., 1967. [see 11, 20, 23, 24, 31, 33, 39, 43; cited 82]

*29. Minneapolis Planning Commission, *Toward a New City*, CRP, Minneapolis, December 1965. [see 4; cited 5, 82]

30. Minneapolis Planning Commission, *Metro Center 1985*, Minneapolis, 1970. [cited 82]

31. Montreal Service d'Urbanisme, *Relevé Visuel: Région de Montréal*, 1967. [see 11, 20, 23, 24, 28, 33, 39, 43]

32. New York City Planning Commission, *New Life for Plazas*, New York, April 1975.

33. Oakland City Planning Department, *Oakland's Form and Appearance*, Oakland, Calif., 1968, and *Design Framework for Oakland*, Oakland, Calif., 1969. [see 11, 20, 23, 24, 28, 31, 39, 43; cited 5, 83]

*34. Okamoto/Liskamm Inc., *Appearance and Design—Principles for the Design and Development of San Francisco Bay*, San Francisco, September 1967. [see 6; cited 71, 83]

35. Okamoto, R., and F. E. Williams, "Urban Design Manhattan," *New York Regional Plan*, Viking, New York, 1969. [see 3, 27; cited 5]

36. Overview Corp., *From the Mountains to the Sea: State of Hawaii Comprehensive Open Space Plan*, for the Department of Planning and Economic Development, Hawaii, 1972, pp. 55-83. [see 16, 18, 41, 44, 49, 50; cited 6, 71, 83]

37. Paju, O., *Regional Miljö: Landskapet, bebyggelsen, våganna; Exempel på skissmaterial Stockholmstraktens Regional Planekontor, 1960-1970*, Regionalplanekontoret, Stockholm, May 1975. [cited 85, 95]

38. Polakowski, K. J., *Upper Great Lakes Regional Recreational Planning Study; Part 5: Scenic Highway System*, Upper Great Lakes Regional Commission, 1974. [see 15, 19, 22, 47; cited 6, 84]

39. Portland Chapter, American Institute of Architects, *Visual Survey of Downtown Portland*, Portland, Ore., April 1971. [see 11, 20, 23, 24, 28, 31, 33, 43; cited 5, 83]

40. Public Art Workshop, *Mural Manual*, Beacon Press, Boston, 1975. [cited 20]

41. Research, Planning and Design, Inc., *Vermont Scenery Classification and Analysis*, report to Vermont State Planning Office, 1971. [see 16, 18, 36, 44, 49, 50; cited 6, 71, 84]

42. Roze, A., et al., *Urban Design with People—A Case Study*, mimeo., Detroit, ca. 1972. [see 14; cited 61, 81]

*43. San Francisco Department of City Planning, *San Francisco Urban Design Study*, eight preliminary reports, and the *Urban Design Plan*, San Francisco, 1969-1971. [see 11, 20, 23, 24, 28, 31, 33, 39; cited 82, 98, 178, 182]

44. Sargent, F. O., *Scenery Classification*, Agricultural Experiment Station, University of Vermont, Burlington, 1971. [see 16, 18, 36, 41, 49, 50; cited 6, 84]

45. Seattle Department of Community Development, *Determinants of City Form*, Urban Design Report No. 1, Seattle, Wash., January 1971. [figs. 27, 40; cited 5, 83]

*46. Southworth, M., and S. Southworth, "Environmental Quality Analysis and Management for Cities and Regions: A Review of the Work in the United States," *Town Planning Review*, July 1973. [cited 81, 86]

47. Steinitz-Rogers Associates, Inc., *Potential Impacts of Interstate 84 in Rhode Island*, Cambridge, Mass., 1972. [see 15, 19, 22, 38; cited 6, 71, 84]

*48. Torrey, I., *Urban Design Mechanisms for San Antonio*, presented at AIP Conference, 1973, mimeo., Torrey and Torrey, San Francisco, Calif. [see 4; cited 57, 81]

49. Vermont Central Planning Office, *Vermont Scenery Preservation*, Montpelier, Vt., 1966. [see 16, 18, 36, 41, 44, 50; cited 6, 71, 84]

*50. Vineyard Open Land Foundation, *Looking at the Vineyard*, West Tisbury, Mass., January 1973. [see 16, 18, 36, 41, 44, 49; figs. 10, 23, 24, 34; cited 71, 83, 92, 106, 114]

51. Vision, Inc., townscape conservation plans for Exeter, N.H., Bellows Falls, Vt., and others; Cambridge, Mass. [cited 71]

52. Weismantel, W., *River of the Mind*, Vol. 3, Citizen Perception Study of the Rio Grande, Center for Environmental Research and Development, University of New Mexico, Albuquerque, 1974. [see 9, 17; cited 115]

A Bibliography of Research

*53. Alexander, C., *A Pattern Language*, Oxford University Press, New York, 1975. [cited 48, 170]

54. Altman, I., *The Environment and Social Behavior*, Brooks/Cole, Monterey, Calif., 1975. [see 63, 88, 89, 96, 169, 180, 197; cited 21, 23, 165, 169, 171]

55. Appleyard, D., "City Design and the Pluralistic City," in L. Rodwin, *Planning Urban Growth and Regional Development*, MIT Press, Cambridge, Mass., 1969. [cited 61, 111, 170]

56. Appleyard, D., and M. Lintell, "The Environmental Quality of the City Street: The Resident's Viewpoint," *Journal of the American Institute of Planners*, Vol. 38 (1972), pp. 84-101. [cited 25, 111]

57. Appleyard, D., K. Lynch, and J. Myer, *The View From the Road*, MIT

Press, Cambridge, Mass., 1964. [see 73, 121, 182, 185; figs. 30, 47; cited 95, 98, 166]

58. Arnheim, R., *Towards a Psychology of Art*, Faber, London, 1967. [cited 14]

59. Babcock, R. F., "Billboards, Glass Houses, and the Law," *Harper's*, April 1966, pp. 20-33.

60. Bachelard, G., *The Poetics of Space*, trans. M. Jolas, Orion Press, New York, 1964. [cited 35, 173]

61. Bacon, E., *Design of Cities*, Viking, New York, 1967. [see 146; cited 5, 90, 168]

62. Banerjee, T. K., "Urban Experience and the Development of the City Image: A Study in Environmental Perception and Learning," Ph.D. Thesis, Department of Urban Studies and Planning, MIT, Cambridge, Mass., 1971. [cited 111, 170]

*63. Barker, R., "On the Nature of Environment," *Journal of Social Issues*, Vol. 24, No. 4 (1963). [see 54, 88, 89, 96, 169, 180, 197]

64. Barker, R., *Ecological Psychology*, Stanford University Press, Stanford, Calif., 1968. [cited 169]

65. Berlyne, D. E., *Aesthetics and Psychobiology*, Appleton-Century-Crofts, New York, 1971. [cited 14, 38]

66. Blumenfeld, H., "Scale in Civic Design," *Town Planning Review*, Vol. 24, No. 1 (April 1953). [cited 90, 168]

67. Boston Children's Museum, "Centre Street: An Exhibit and Fair," Children's Museum, Jamaica Plain, Mass., 1975. [cited 32, 174]

68. Brodey, W., "The Other-than-Visual World of the Blind," *Architectural Design*, January 1969. [cited 167]

69. Brower, S., "The Signs We Learn to Read," *Landscape*, Autumn 1965. [cited 23]

70. Carr, S., "The City of the Mind," *Environment for Man*, W. R. Ewald (ed.) Indiana University Press, Bloomington, 1967. [cited 170]

*71. Carr, S., et al., *Ecologue/Cambridgeport Project*, final report, Department of Urban Studies and Planning, MIT, Cambridge, Mass., December 1972, for Office for Environmental Education, U.S. Department of Health, Education, and Welfare. [fig. 51; cited 63, 111, 174]

72. Carr, S., and K. Lynch, "Where Learning Happens," *Daedalus*, Vol. 97, No. 4, (Fall 1968). [cited 32, 174]

73. Carr, S., and D. Schissler, "The City as a Trip: Perceptual Selection and Memory in the View from the Road," *Environment and Behavior*, June 1969. [see 57, 121, 182, 185; cited 166]

74. Civic Trust, "Pride of Place," London, 1972. [cited 23]

75. Collier, J., *Visual Anthropology: Photography as a Research Method*, Holt, Rinehart, and Winston, New York, 1967. [cited 108]

76. Coomber, N. C., and D. Biswas, *Evaluating Environmental Intangibles*, Geneva Press, Bronxville, N.Y., 1973. [cited 14]

77. Cooper, C., *Some Social Implications of House and Site Plan Design in Easter Village*, Institute of Urban and Regional Development, University of California, Berkeley, 1965.

*78. Cooper, C., *The House as a Symbol of Self*, Institute of Urban and Regional Development, University of California, Berkeley, 1971. [see 127; cited 23, 35, 173]

79. Coughlin, R. E., and K. A. Goldstein, *The Extent of Agreement Among Observers on Environmental Attractiveness*, Regional Science Research Institute, Discussion Paper No. 37, Philadelphia, February 1970. [see 101, 163; cited 14, 173]

80. Craik, K., "The Comprehension of the Everyday Physical Environment," *Journal of the American Institute of Planners*, Vol. 34 (January 1968). [cited 113]

*81. Cullen, G., *The Concise Townscape*, Van Nostrand, New York, 1971. [see 105, 106, 125, 143, 155; cited 23, 168]

82. Downs, R. M., and D. Stea, *Image and Environment: Cognitive Mapping and Spatial Behavior*, Aldine, Chicago, 1973. [see 90; cited 23, 111, 170]

83. Edney, J. J., "Human Territories as Organizers: Some Social and Psychological Consequences of Attachment to Place," *Environment and Behavior*, Vol. 8, No. 1 (March 1976). [cited 21, 171]

84. Fruin, J. J., *Pedestrian Planning and Design*, Metropolitan Association of Urban Designers and Environmental Planners, New York, 1971. [cited 16, 169]

85. Gibson, J. J., *The Perception of the Visual World*, Houghton Mifflin, Boston, 1950. [cited 14]

86. Glacken, C. J., *Traces on the Rhodian Shore*, University of California Press, Berkeley, 1967. [cited 35, 172]

87. Glaser, B. J. and A. L. Straus, "Discovery of Grounded Theory," in W. J. Filstead (ed.), *Qualitative Methodology*, Markham, Chicago, 1970.

88. Goffman, E., *The Presentation of Self in Everyday Life*, Doubleday, New York, 1959. [see 54, 63, 96, 169, 180, 197]

89. Goffman, E., *Behavior in Public Places*, Free Press, New York, 1963. [see 54, 63, 88, 96, 169, 180, 197; cited 169]

*90. Golledge, R. G., and R. Moore, *Environmental Knowing*, Dowden, Hutchinson and Ross, Inc., Stroudsburg, Pa. (forthcoming). [see 82; cited 23, 111, 112, 113, 170, 172]

*91. Goodey, B., *Perception of the Environment*, Center for Urban and Regional Studies, Occasional Paper No. 17, University of Birmingham, England, 1971. [cited 111, 170]

92. Goodey, B., *A Checklist of Sources on Environmental Perception*, Research Memorandum No. 11, Center for Urban and Regional Studies, University of Birmingham, England, March 1972. [cited 170]

93. Goodey, B., *Images of Place: Essays on Environmental Perception, Com-*

munications, and Education, Center for Urban and Regional Studies, University of Birmingham, England, 1974. [cited 23, 174]

94. Goodey, B., *City Scene: An Exploration into the Image of Central Birmingham as Seen by Area Residents*, Research Memorandum No. 10, Center for Urban and Regional Studies, University of Birmingham, England, 1971. [cited 61, 112]

*95. Grandjean, E., *Fitting the Task to the Man: An Ergonomic Approach*, Taylor and Francis, London, 1971. [cited 15, 16, 168]

*96. Grey, A. L., et al., *People and Downtown*, University of Washington, Seattle, September 1970. [see 54, 63, 88, 89, 169, 180, 197; fig. 4; cited 169]

97. Hack, G., *Improving the City Streets for Use at Night: The Norfolk Experiment*, Department of Urban Studies and Planning, MIT, Cambridge, Mass., June 1974. [cited 19, 20, 167]

98. Harrison, J. D., *The Perception and Cognition of Environment*, annotated exchange bibliography No. 516, Council of Planning Librarians, Monticello, Ill., January 1974. [cited 170]

99. Harrison, J. D., and W. A. Howard, "The Role of Meaning in the Urban Image," *Environment and Behavior*, Vol. 4, No. 4 (December 1972). [cited 113]

100. Heath, T., *Environmental Aesthetics, The State of the Art*, Royal Australian Institute of Architects Research Report, Copper and Brass Information Centre, Sydney, 1975. [see 192; cited 14]

101. Herzog, T. R., Kaplan, and Kaplan, "The Prediction of Preference for Familiar Urban Places," *Environment and Behavior*, forthcoming. [see 79, 163]

102. Hopkinson, R. G., "The Quantitative Assessment of Visual Intrusion," *Journal of the Town Planning Institute*, Vol. 7, No. 10 (1971). [cited 15, 100, 167]

*103. Hubbard, H. V., and T. Kimball, *An Introduction to the Study of Landscape Design*, Macmillan, New York, 1924. [cited 168]

*104. Ittelson, W. H., et al., *An Introduction to Environmental Psychology*, Holt, Rinehart and Winston, New York, 1974. [see 150; cited 165]

105. Jackson, J. B., *Landscapes*, ed. E. H. Zube, University of Massachusetts Press, Amherst, 1970. [see 81, 106, 125, 143, 155; cited 172, 173]

106. Jackson, J. B., *American Space*, Norton, New York, 1972. [see 81, 105, 125, 143, 155]

107. Kates, R. W., and J. F. Wohlwill (eds.), "Man's Response to the Physical Environment," *Journal of Social Issues*, Vol. 22, No. 4 (1966), pp. 1-140.

108. Kazin, A., *A Walker in the City*, Grove Press, New York, 1951. [cited 35]

109. Kepes, G., "Notes on Expression and Communication in the Cityscape," *Daedalus*, Winter 1961. [cited 35, 168]

110. Klein, H., "The Delineation of the Town Centre in the Image of its Citizens," in E. J. Brill (ed.), *Urban Core and Inner City*, University of Amsterdam, Leiden, 1967. [cited 111, 170]

111. Ladd, F. C., "Black Youths View Their Neighborhood: Neighborhood Maps," *Environment and Behavior*, Vol. 2 (1970), pp. 74-99. [cited 23, 35, 111, 170]

112. Lassiere, A., *The Environmental Evaluation of Transport Plans at the Strategy Level*, Department of the Environment, London, England, October 1974. [cited 85, 184]

113. Lee, T. R., "Perceived Distance as a Function of Direction in the City," *Environment and Behavior*, Vol. 2 (1970), pp. 40-51. [cited 111]

114. Leighty, L., "Aesthetics as a Legal Basis for Environmental Control," *17 Wayne Law Review*, 1971. [cited 40]

115. Leopold, L., "Landscape Aesthetics," *Ekistics*, April 1970.

116. Lerup, L., "Environmental and Behavioral Congruence as a Measure of Goodness in Public Space: The Case of Stockholm," *DMG-DRS Journal*, Vol. 6, No. 2 (April/June 1972). [cited 19]

117. Leuba, C., "The Concept of Optimal Stimulation," in H. Fowler, *Curiosity and Exploratory Behavior*, Macmillan, New York, 1965. [cited 14]

118. Lewis, O., *The Children of Sanchez*, Random House, New York, 1961. [cited 35]

119. Lewis, P. F., D. Lowenthal, and Y. Tuan, *Visual Blight in America*, Association of American Geographers Research Paper No. 23, 1973.

120. Ling, A., "Skyscrapers and Their Siting in Cities," *Town Planning Review*, Vol. 34, No. 1 (April 1963). [see 21, 123, 145; cited 178]

121. Little, Arthur D., Inc., *Response to Roadside Environment*, Outdoor Advertising Association of America, 1968. [see 57, 73, 182, 185; cited 174]

122. Litton, R. B., *Forest Landscape Description and Inventories*, U.S. Department of Agriculture, Forest Service Research Paper PSW-49, 1968. [cited 92]

123. Litton, R. B., *Landscape Control Points*, U.S. Department of Agriculture, Forest Service Research Paper PSW-91, 1973. [see 21, 120, 145; fig. 38; cited 100, 184]

124. Lowenthal, D., "Geography, Experience, and Imagination," *Annals*, American Association of Geographers, September 1961. [cited 113]

125. Lowenthal, D., and H. C. Prince, "English Landscape Tastes," *Geographical Review*, Vol. 55 (April 1965). [see 81, 105, 106, 143, 155; cited 173]

126. Lowenthal, D., and M. Riel, *Publications in Environmental Perception*, Nos. 1-8, American Geographical Society, New York, 1972. (Eight pamphlets: environmental assessments of New York, Boston, Cambridge, and Columbus and a comparative analysis; structures of environmental association; milieu and observer differences; and semantic and experiential components.) [cited 14, 111, 113, 166]

*127. Lukashok, A., and K. Lynch, "Some Childhood Memories of the City," *Journal of the American Institute of Planners*, Vol. 22, No. 3 (Summer 1956). [cited 23, 111]

*128. Lynch, K., *The Image of the City*, MIT Press, Cambridge, Mass., 1960. [see 168; cited 23, 29, 61, 111, 170]

129. Lynch, K., "The Openness of Open Space," Chapt. 1, in *Open Space for Human Needs*, Marcou, O'Leary and Associates, Washington, D.C., 1970. [cited 27]

130. Lynch, K., *Site Planning*, 2d edition, MIT Press, Cambridge, Mass., 1971. [cited 168]

*131. Lynch, K., *What Time Is This Place?*, MIT Press, Cambridge, Mass., 1972. [cited 28, 30, 94, 171, 189]

132. Lynch, K., *Growing Up in Cities: Studies of the Spatial Environment of Adolescents in Cracow, Melbourne, Mexico City, Salta, Toluca and Warszawa*, Report for UNESCO, 1975. [see 134; figs. 7, 45; cited 14, 32, 111, 169]

133. Lynch, K., and M. Rivkin, "A Walk Around the Block," *Landscape*, Vol. 8, No. 3 (Spring 1959). [cited 111]

134. Mauer, R., and J. C. Baxter, "Images of the Neighborhood and City among Black-, Anglo-, and Mexican-American Children," *Environment and Behavior*, Vol. 4 (1972), pp. 351-388. [see 132; cited 32, 111]

135. Michelson, W., *Man and His Urban Environment*, Addison-Wesley, Reading, Mass., 1970. [cited 172]

136. Milgram, S., "The Experience of Living in Cities," *Science*, Vol. 167 (1970), pp. 1461-1468. [cited 111, 169]

137. Miller, G. A., "The Magical Number Seven Plus or Minus Two: Some Limits on Our Capacity for Processing Information," *Psychological Review*, Vol. 63 (1956), pp. 81-97. [cited 14]

138. Miller, G. A., E. Galanter, and K. Pribam, *Plans and the Structure of Behavior*, Holt, New York, 1960.

139. Miller, J. D., *Effects of Noise on People*, Central Institute for the Deaf, for the U.S. Environmental Protection Agency, U.S. Government Printing Office, Washington, D.C., December 1971. [cited 15, 167]

140. MIT Department of Urban Studies and Planning, *Signs in the City*, Cambridge, Mass., June 1963, reprinted by the Laboratory for Environmental Studies, MIT, Cambridge, Mass., March 1971. [fig. 43; cited 30, 105, 174, 193]

141. Moore, R., *The Ecology of a Neighborhood Playground: Implications for Planning, Design and Management*, Department of Landscape Architecture, University of California, Berkeley, 1973. [cited 174]

142. Muchow, M. and H., *Der Lebensraum des Grosstadt Kindes*, Hamburg, M. Riegel, 1935. [cited 169]

143. Nairn, I., *The American Landscape, A Critical View*, Random House, New York, 1965. [see 81, 105, 106, 125, 155; cited 23, 91, 96, 168]

*144. Neutra, R., and R. A. McFarland, "Accident Epidemology and the Design of the Residential Environment," *Human Factors*, Vol. 14 (1972), pp. 405-420. [cited 15]

145. Parke, M., *View Protection Regulations*, American Society of Planning Officials, Planning Advisory Service Report No. 213, Chicago, 1966. [see 21, 120, 123; cited 179]

146. Peets, E., *On the Art of Designing Cities*, ed. P. Spreiregen MIT Press, Cambridge, Mass., 1968. [see 56; cited 5, 168]

147. Petersen, J. T., *The Climate of Cities: A Survey of Recent Literature*, National Air Pollution Control Administration, U.S. Department of Health, Education, and Welfare, Raleigh, N.C., 1969. [cited 19, 101]

*148. Perin, C., *With Man in Mind*, MIT Press, Cambridge, Mass., 1972. [cited 110, 170]

*149. Piaget, J., *The Child's Conception of the World*, Routledge and Kegan Paul, London, 1964. [cited 170, 174]

*150. Proshansky, H. H., W. H. Ittelson, and L. G. Rivlin (eds.), *Environmental Psychology: Man and His Physical Setting*, 2d Edition, Holt, Rinehart, and Winston, New York, 1976. [see 104; cited 165]

151. Rainwater, L., "Fear and the House-as-Haven in the Lower Class," *Journal of the American Institute of Planners*, January 1965. [cited 113]

152. Rand, G., "Pre-Copernican Views of the City," *Architectural Forum*, Vol. 131 (September 1969).

*153. Rapoport, A., "Observations Regarding Man-Environment Systems," *Man/Environment Systems*, January 1970. [cited 14, 165, 170]

154. Rapoport, A., and R. Hawkes, "The Perception of Urban Complexity," *Journal of the American Institute of Planners*, March 1970. [cited 174]

155. Rasmussen, S. E., *Towns and Buildings*, Harvard University Press, Cambridge, Mass., 1951. [see 81, 105, 106, 125, 143; cited 168]

156. Reynolds, I., and C. Nicholson, *The Estate Outside the Dwelling*, Department of the Environment, Great Britain, Her Majesty's Stationery Office, London, 1972. [cited 172]

157. Rivlin, L. G., and M. Wolfe, "The Early History of a Psychiatric Hospital for Children," *Environment and Behavior*, Vol. 4, No. 1 (March 1972). [cited 169]

158. Robinette, G. O., *Plants, People and Environmental Quality*, U.S. Government Printing Office, Washington, D.C., #2405-0479. [see 161; cited 106]

159. Royse, D., *Social Inferences via Environmental Clues*, Ph.D. Thesis, Department of Urban Studies and Planning, MIT, Cambridge, Mass., 1969. [cited 113, 171]

160. Rudofsky, B., *Streets for People: A Primer for Americans*, Doubleday, Garden City, N.Y., 1969. [cited 168]

161. Schmid, J. A., *Urban Vegetation, A Review and Chicago Case Study*, Chicago University Department of Geography, 1974. [see 158; cited 106]

162. Searles, H. F., *The Non-Human Environment*, International University Press, New York, 1960. [cited 35, 167, 173]

163. Shafer, E. L., and M. Tooby, "Landscape Preferences: An International Replication," *Journal of Leisure Research*, Vol. 5, No. 3 (1973), pp. 60-65. [see 81, 101; cited 14, 173]

164. Sieverts, T., "Perceptual Images of the City of Berlin," E. J. Brill (ed.), *Urban Core and Inner City*, University of Amsterdam, Leiden, 1967. [cited 111, 170]

165. Simmel, G., "The Metropolis and Mental Life," in P. K. Hatt and A. J. Reiss (eds.), *Reader in Urban Life*, Free Press, New York, 1951.

166. Sims, W., *Neighborhoods: Columbus Neighborhood Definitions Study*, Columbus, Ohio, 1973. [cited 111, 112, 171]

167. Sims, W., "Iconic Simulations: An Evaluation of Their Effectiveness as Techniques for Simulating Environmental Experience along Cognitive Affective, and Behavioral Dimensions," Ph.D. Thesis, Department of Urban Studies and Planning, MIT, Cambridge, Mass., September 1974. [see 171; cited 91, 170]

168. Smith, B. A., "The Image of the City 10 Years Later," MCP Thesis, MIT, Department of Urban Studies and Planning, Cambridge, Mass., 1969. [see 128; cited 170]

*169. Sommer, R., *Personal Space: The Behavioral Basis of Design*, Prentice-Hall, Englewood Cliffs, N.J., 1969. [see 54, 63, 88, 96, 180, 197; cited 21, 169]

170. Sommer, R., *Design Awareness*, Holt, Rinehart and Winston, New York, 1972. [cited 14, 20]

171. Sorte, G. J., "Methods for Presenting Planned Environments," *Man/Environment Systems*, Vol. 5 (May 1975), pp. 148-154. [see 167; cited 166]

172. Southworth, M., *The Sonic Environment of Cities*, MIT, Cambridge, Mass., 1967. [fig. 41; cited 14, 102, 167]

173. Southworth, M., "An Urban Service for Children Based on an Analysis of Cambridgeport Boys' Conception and Use of the City," Ph.D. Thesis, MIT, Cambridge, Mass., 1970. [cited 111, 169]

174. Southworth, M., and K. Lynch, *Designing and Managing the Strip*, Joint Center for Urban Studies of MIT and Harvard University, Working Paper No. 29, Cambridge, Mass., October 1974. [cited 104, 188]

175. Stea, D., and R. Downs, "From the Outside Looking In at the Inside Looking Out," *Environment and Behavior*, Vol. 2, No. 1 (June 1970). [cited 111, 170]

176. Stea, D., and D. Wood, *Un Atlas Cognitivo: La Geografia Psicologica de Cuatro Ciudades Mexicanes*, 1970. [cited 23, 111, 170]

177. Steinitz, C., "Congruence and Meaning: The Influence of Consistency between Urban Form and Activity on Environmental Knowledge," Ph.D. Thesis, MIT, Cambridge, Mass., 1967. [cited 170]

178. Stokols, D. (ed.), *Psychological Perspectives on Environment and Behavior: Conceptual and Empirical Trends*, Plenum, New York, in press. [cited 170, 172]

*179. Strauss, A., *The American City: A Sourcebook of Urban Imagery*, Aldine, Chicago, 1968. [cited 111]

*180. Suttles, G. D., *The Social Order of the Slum: Ethnicity and Territory in the Inner City*, University of Chicago Press, 1968. [see 54, 63, 88, 89, 96, 169, 197; cited 21, 23]

181. Svenson, E., "Differential Perception and Behavioral Response to Change in Urban Spatial Form, Ph.D. Thesis, MIT, Cambridge, Mass., 1967. [cited 171]

182. Thiel, P., "A Sequence-Experience Notation," *Town Planning Review*, Vol. 32, No. 1 (April 1961). [see 57, 73, 121, 185; cited 98]

183. Trieb, M., *Stadtgestaltung, Theorie und Praxis*, Bertelsman Fachverlag, Düsseldorf, 1974. [fig. 19]

*184. Tuan, Yi-Fu, *Topophilia: A Study of Environmental Attitudes, Perceptions, and Values*, Prentice-Hall, Englewood Cliffs, N.J., 1974. [cited 35]

185. Tunnard, C., and B. Pushkarev, *Man-Made America, Chaos or Control?*, Yale University Press, New Haven, 1963 (esp. the chapter on rural highways). [see 57, 73, 121, 182; cited 95]

186. Ure, P. N., *Justinian and His Age*, Penguin, Harmondsworth, 1951, pp. 164-165. [cited 184]

187. U.S. Departments of Interior and Agriculture, *Environmental Criteria for Electric Transmission Systems*, U.S. Government Printing Office, Washington, D.C.

188. Van der Ryn, S. H., *Amenity Attributes of Residential Locations*, Technical Paper No. 3, CRP, San Francisco, May 1965. [cited 14, 172]

189. Van der Ryn, S. H., and W. R. Boie, *Value Measurement and Visual Factors in the Urban Environment*, College of Environmental Design, University of California, Berkeley, January 1963, mimeo.

190. Varming, M., *Motorveje i Landskabet*, Statens Byggeforskningsinstitut, Copenhagen, 1970. [cited 95]

191. Walters, D., "Annoyance Due to Railway Noise in Residential Locations," in *Architectural Psychology*, RIBA, London, 1969. [cited 15]

192. Washington Environmental Research Center, for the U.S. Environmental Protection Agency, *Aesthetics in Environmental Planning*, EPA 600/5-73-009, U.S. Government Printing Office, Washington, D.C., November 1963. [see 100]

193. Weiss, R. S., and S. Boutourline, *Fairs, Pavilions, Exhibits and Their Audiences*, mimeo., 1962. [cited 169]

194. Whyte, W. H., "The Best Street Life in the World: Why Schmoozing, Smooching, Noshing, Ogling are Getting Better All the Time," *New York Magazine*, July 15, 1974. [cited 108, 110]

195. Wilson, R. L., "Livability of the City: Attitudes and Urban Develop-

ment," in F. S. Chapin and S. F. Weiss (eds.), *Urban Growth Dynamics*, Wiley, New York, 1962. [cited 14, 172]

196. Wohlwill, J. F., and D. H. Carson (eds.), *Environment and the Social Sciences: Perspectives and Applications*, American Psychological Association, Washington, D.C., 1972. [cited 165]

197. Zeisel, J., *Sociology and Architectural Design*, Russell Sage, New York, 1974. [see 54, 63, 88, 89, 96, 169, 180; cited 165, 169]

198. Zube, E. H., "Scenery as a Natural Resource: Implications of Public Policy, and Problems of Definition, Description, and Evaluation," *Landscape Architecture*, Vol. 63, No. 2 (1973). [cited 173]

199. Zube, E. H., R. O. Brush, and J. G. Fabos, *Landscape Assessment: Values, Perceptions, and Resources*, Dowden, Hutchinson and Ross, Stroudsburg, Pa., 1975. [cited 14, 115, 172, 173]

Journals of Special Interest

Environment and Behavior, G. Winkel (ed.), Sage Publications, Beverly Hills, Calif.

Man/Environment Systems, A. H. Esser (ed.), Asmer, Inc., Orangeburg, N.Y.

Architectural Psychology Newsletter, Architectural Psychology Research Unit, School of Architecture, Kingston Polytechnic, Kingston-upon-Thames, Surrey, England.

Addenda

Bibliography of Examples

200. Carney, W., *Trees for Cincinnati*, The Cincinnati Institute for the Wilder Foundation, Cincinnati, Ohio, 1975.

201. Cincinnati Institute, *Cincinnati Hillsides: Development Guidelines*, Cincinnati, Ohio, December 1975.

202. Clark, R. S., "A Case Study: Seattle's Citywide Design Commission," *Practicing Planner*, Vol. 6, No. 1 (February 1976), pp. 32-39.

203. Dallas Department of Planning and Development, *Design Guideline for Inner City Neighborhoods*, Dallas, Tex., July 1972.

204. Perlman, B., "1% Art in Civic Architecture," RTKL Associates, Baltimore, Md., 1973.

205. Urban Design Council, *Housing Quality: A Program for Zoning Reform*, New York City, 1973.

Bibliography of Research

206. Fairbrother, N., *New Lives, New Landscapes*, Knopf, New York, 1970.

207. Firey, W., "Sentiment and Symbolism as Ecological Variables," in G. A. Theodorson (ed.), *Studies in Human Ecology*, Harper and Row, New York, 1961.

208. Hall, E., "Proxemics: The Study of Man's Spatial Relations," in I. Galdston (ed.), *Man's Image in Medicine and Anthropology*, International Universities Press, New York, 1963.

209. Lu, W., *The Urban Design Role in Local Government* (preliminary report of a conference), Goals for Dallas, Dallas, Texas, July 1976.

210. Lynch, K., "Urban Design," *Encyclopedia Brittanica*, 15th Edition, Volume 18, pp. 1053-1065, Encyclopedia Brittanica, Inc., Chicago, 1974.

211. Moss, S., "A Policy for the Visual Form of Industrial Areas," MCP Thesis, Department of Urban Studies and Planning, Massachusetts Institute of Technology, Cambridge, Mass., 1964.

212. Schwartz, R., "Subway of the Mind," *Connection*, Fall 1967.

213. Sitte, C., *The Art of Building Cities*, trans. Charles T. Stewart, Reinhold, New York, 1945 (orig. 1889).

214. Ulrich, R. S., *Scenery and the Shopping Trip: The Roadside Environment as a Factor in Route Choice*, Michigan Geographical Publication No. 12, Department of Geography, University of Michigan, Ann Arbor, 1974.

215. Wejchert, K., *Elementy Kompozycji Urbanistycznej*, Wydawnictwo Arkady, Warszawa, 1974.

Credits

1a   Title Insurance Company, San Diego, California.

1b   Bill Reid, *San Diego Magazine.*

2a-f   K. Lynch and D. Appleyard, *Temporary Paradise?* Planning Department, City of San Diego, 1974.

3   Nishan Bichajian.

4   A. L. Grey et al., *People and Downtown.* Seattle: University of Washington Press, 1970. (Department of Health, Education and Welfare Urban Renewal Demonstration Grant No. Wash D-1.)

5   D. Appleyard, "Street Livability Study," in *San Francisco Urban Design Study*, San Francisco, 1969.

6   City Planning Commission, *The Visual Environment of Los Angeles.* Los Angeles, April 1971.

7   From a study by M. Susułowska and M. Sawicki, reproduced in K. Lynch, *Growing Up in Cities.* UNESCO (forthcoming).

8   A. Kutcher, *The New Jerusalem.* Cambridge, Mass.: MIT Press, 1975.

9   Robin Moore.

10   Vineyard Open Land Foundation, *Looking at the Vineyard.* West Tisbury, Massachusetts, January 1973.

11   Commission Intercommunale d'Urbanisme, *Plan Directeur de la Région Lausannoise, Analyse des sites et aspects pratiques de leur protection.* Lausanne, Switzerland, 1970.

12   Detroit City Planning Commission, *Detroit 1990: An Urban Design Concept for the Inner City.* Detroit, 1971.

13   Office of Lower Manhattan Development, City of New York.

14   Design by D. Appleyard, from Lynch and Appleyard, *Temporary Paradise?*

15   G. T. Nolli, Plan of Rome, 1748.

16   E. Bacon, reproduced in M. Trieb, *Stadtgestaltung: Theorie und Praxis.* Düsseldorf: Bertelsmann Fachverlag, 1974.

17   Kutcher, *The New Jerusalem.*

18   Kutcher, *The New Jerusalem.*

19   Freie Planungsgruppe Berlin, reproduced in Trieb, *Stadtgestaltung: Theorie und Praxis.*

20   Richard Peterson, Aptos Village, California.

21,22   K. Lynch, *Visual Analysis*, Community Renewal Program, Brookline, Massachusetts, September 1965.

23,24   Vineyard Open Land Foundation, *Looking at the Vineyard.*

25   C. Steinitz, "Congruence and Meaning," Ph.D. Thesis, Department of Urban Studies and Planning, MIT, 1967.

26   Historic Savannah Foundation, Inc.

27   Seattle Department of Community Development, *Determinants of City Form.*

28   Drawn by Jack Schnitzius for Okamoto and Liskamm, San Francisco.

29   D. Appleyard, College of Environmental Design, University of California, Berkeley.

30   D. Appleyard, K. Lynch, and J. Myer, *The View from the Road.* Cambridge, Mass.: MIT Press, 1964.

31   Philip Thiel, "A Sequence-Experience Notation," *Town Planning Review*, April 1961.

32   Okamoto and Liskamm, *San Francisco Urban Design Study*, 1970.

33   Kutcher, *The New Jerusalem.*

34   Vineyard Open Land Foundation, *Looking at the Vineyard.*

35,36   Kutcher, *The New Jerusalem.*

37   Drawing by Norman Klein, 1953.

38   R. Litton, "Landscape Control Points," USDA Forest Service Research Paper PSW 91/1973.

39   Redrawn from T. J. Chandler, *The Climate of London.* London: Hutchinson and Co., Ltd., 1965.

40   Seattle Department of Community Development, *Determinants of City Form.*

41   M. Southworth, "The Sonic Environment of Cities," *Environment and Behavior*, June 1969.

42   MIT Planning Office.

43   MIT Department of Urban Studies and Planning, "Signs in the City," 1971.

44   A. Gerstenberger, "Strategies for Improving the Night Environment," MCP Thesis, Department of Urban Studies and Planning, MIT, June 1974.

45   From a study by Peter Downton, Melbourne, Australia, reproduced in K. Lynch, *Growing Up in Cities*, UNESCO, (forthcoming).

46   City Planning Commission, Los Angeles, *The Visual Environment of Los Angeles.*

47 Appleyard, Lynch, and Myer, *The View from the Road.*

48,49 K. Lynch, *Visual Analysis.*

50 Arrowstreet, Inc. (formerly Ashley/Myer/Smith, Inc.), Cambridge, Massachusetts.

51 S. Carr et al., "Ecologue/Cambridgeport Project," final report, December 1972, Office of Environmental Education, U.S. Department of Health, Education and Welfare, Washington, D.C.

52 Jones and Jones, *Scenic and Recreational Highway Study,* for the Legislative Transportation Committee, State of Washington, 1974.

53 Greater London Council, Department of Architecture and Civic Design, *Thames-side Environmental Assessment,* London, March 1968.

54 Kutcher, *The New Jerusalem.*

55 K. Lynch, *Visual Analysis.*

56 Kutcher, *The New Jerusalem.*

Acknowledgments

I am unable to list, or to remember, all those whom I have drawn upon in writing this book. It is a summary of the work of many persons. Michael Southworth made the first survey of American experience in sensory management, and I have used that survey extensively. Anne Washington kept me organized and moving forward. Graduate students at M.I.T. continue to deepen and correct my ideas. Donald Appleyard, Stephen Call, and Weiming Lu are colleagues who have steadily been productive in this field. I have reflected their ideas and experiences repeatedly here, and likely at times distorted them. I would also like to remember Norman Klein, who devoted his life to improving the sense of our cities.

Index